"I'm so grateful to finally have a clear, informative, and helpful introductory resource to help God's people faithfully interpret Scripture. In *Understanding God's Word*, Jon Nielson provides six "tools" that give contours to hermeneutical application for the pastor and layperson alike. This volume will undoubtedly be my go-to recommendation for anybody wanting to rightly and accurately interpret the Bible!"

Brian Cosby, Senior Pastor, Wayside Presbyterian Church, Signal Mountain, Tennessee; Adjunct Professor of Historical Theology, Reformed Theological Seminary, Atlanta

"These principles have transformed the way I personally read, understand, and teach God's word. I have been using them for over a decade and cannot recommend them highly enough. Jon clearly explains each principle using language we can all understand, working through multiple examples so we can practice and develop our own muscles. At the end of each chapter, I find myself confident and excited to keep trying. I pray this book will encourage many to dig into God's word, producing fruit and life transformation. I can't wait to use this in our church. What a fantastic resource!"

Abi Byrd, Ministry Associate, McLean Bible Church, Arlington, Virginia; Women's Instructor, The Charles Simeon Trust; author, *You Stand in Grace: Devotions for Walking in Faith* (forthcoming)

"What a clear and useful book! It will help anyone who reads the Bible. And for those who teach the Bible—study leaders, children's class volunteers, parents training their kids—this book is a must-read. Give it to every teacher in your church. It's easy to follow and full of wisdom."

Jack Klumpenhower, author, *Show Them Jesus*

"This is the book I wish I'd had twenty years ago! Jon Nielson has written an accessible guidebook to learning how to soundly interpret the Bible. The six interpretation tools and the opportunities to practice using them are invaluable and set this book apart. As one who teaches others how to study and teach the Bible, I cannot wait to recommend this book and add it to my library."

Colleen D. Searcy, Bible teacher; speaker; creator, Meet Me in the Bible resources

"The third volume in Jon Nielson's excellent series Theology Basics lives up to the same standard set in the earlier books. This time Nielson aims to help the reader properly understand the Scriptures. What a vital subject for the church! *Understanding God's Word* is a master class on how to make the complexity of proper biblical hermeneutics accessible to a wide readership. Here is a toolbox that serves to equip Christians to read and understand the Bible on its terms. Nielson takes up and explains the classic categories for proper biblical interpretation, such as identifying the passage's context, its core emphasis, and its relation to Christ. This is a book suited both for individual and group study, with each section accompanied by suggested verses for memory and guides for praying. Like the first two volumes in this series, I will be enthusiastically commending *Understanding God's Word* to the men and women I serve as pastor."

Todd Pruitt, Pastor, Covenant Presbyterian Church, Harrisonburg, Virginia; Cohost, *Mortification of Spin*

"In *Understanding God's Word,* Jon Nielson provides a thoughtful and practical introduction to rightly handling the Bible. Written with great clarity, each chapter introduces a tool that will stir up the reader to make progress in reading, understanding, and applying the Bible. This book gives needed training that will help Bible readers feast on God's word for a lifetime."

Ben Panner, Director of Workshops, The Charles Simeon Trust, Chicago

UNDERSTANDING GOD'S WORD

The Theology Basics Series by Jon Nielson

Knowing God's Truth: An Introduction to Systematic Theology

Knowing God's Truth Workbook: An Introduction to Systematic Theology

Tracing God's Story: An Introduction to Biblical Theology

Tracing God's Story Workbook: An Introduction to Biblical Theology

Understanding God's Word: An Introduction to Interpreting the Bible

Understanding God's Word Workbook: An Introduction to Interpreting the Bible

UNDERSTANDING GOD'S WORD

An Introduction to Interpreting the Bible

JON NIELSON

CROSSWAY®

WHEATON, ILLINOIS

Understanding God's Word: An Introduction to Interpreting the Bible

Published by Crossway
1300 Crescent Street
Wheaton, Illinois 60187

Cover design: Zach DeYoung

First printing 2025

Printed in Colombia

All emphases in Scripture quotations have been added by the author.

Hardcover ISBN: 978-1-4335-8743-6
ePub ISBN: 978-1-4335-8746-7
PDF ISBN: 978-1-4335-8744-3

Library of Congress Cataloging-in-Publication Data

Names: Nielson, Jon, 1983- author.
Title: Understanding God's word: an introduction to interpreting the Bible / Jon Nielson.
Description: Wheaton, Illinois: Crossway, 2025. | Series: Theology basics series | Includes index. | Summary: "This book will serve to introduce teens (and perhaps laypeople) to basic tools and principles for studying the Bible and understanding it rightly—in its original context and with proper application for today. Its goal will be to equip young believers to approach God's word as faithful students—both to study and begin to communicate its truth clearly."—Provided by publisher.
Identifiers: LCCN 2024005050 (print) | LCCN 2024005051 (ebook) | ISBN 9781433587436 (hardcover) | ISBN 9781433587443 (pdf) | ISBN 9781433587467 (epub)
Subjects: LCSH: Bible—Study and teaching—Juvenile literature.
Classification: LCC BS546 .N65 2025 (print) | LCC BS546 (ebook) | DDC 220.6/1—dc23/eng/20240708
LC record available at https://lccn.loc.gov/2024005050
LC ebook record available at https://lccn.loc.gov/2024005051

Crossway is a publishing ministry of Good News Publishers.

NP 33 32 31 30 29 28 27 26 25
14 13 12 11 10 9 8 7 6 5 4 3 2 1

For my daughters,
Adelyn, Averie, Emilie, and Lucy.
May you know, believe, and obey
the good word
of our great God.

CONTENTS

INTRODUCTION

For many years, Pastor Dick Lucas (St. Helen's Bishopsgate Church in London) taught pastors his "Lucas Lessons"—principles for exposition that are foundational for studying God's word, finding the correct main point and main application, and preaching the text faithfully to God's people. I'm proud to say that I have a binder full of these Lucas Lessons, passed down to me from my father, who sat under some of Pastor Lucas's lessons along with the rest of the College Church pastoral staff in the late 1990s. Several of the most important lessons serve as the launching points for the "tools" that I'll explain and apply throughout this book. This training ministry of Pastor Lucas ultimately launched the Proclamation Trust, which still provides wonderful word training to men and women in London for the good of the local church around the world.

Pastor David Helm (Christ Church Chicago), who founded the Charles Simeon Trust (an organization that trains preachers worldwide in expository word ministry), adapted several of the Lucas Lessons into what CST instructors now teach as "principles of exposition." I had the great privilege of working under David at the Charles Simeon Trust, and I have served as an instructor at several of their national workshops. The CST principles of exposition also undergird and shape the tools that, in the following pages, I seek to explain and apply for laypeople in their study of Scripture. I'm grateful to say that I shared the vision for this book with David several months before working on the manuscript, and he enthusiastically offered his support for my adaptation of the CST principles for this purpose. Men and women who read this book after attending CST workshops around the world will certainly hear familiar emphases and instructions.

Those familiar with other organizations that have been influenced by the word training of Dick Lucas, the Proclamation Trust, and the Charles Simeon Trust will hear many echoes of their principles for faithful preaching, which I'm now applying more broadly to Bible study, interpretation, and application.

All of this is to say that the tools that make up the content of this book are part of a wonderful tradition of pastoral training—from Pastor Dick Lucas and his Lucas Lessons to Pastor David Helm and the Charles Simeon Trust to the training work of many organizations and ministries all over the world. It's my delight to adapt and utilize these wonderful tools to aid young and growing Christians in their interpretation and application of God's word. These tools have been incredibly helpful to me, and I hope they will help you as well.

Before we begin, let me say a word about the organization of the chapters. Here's what you should be ready for:

- Near the beginning of each chapter, you'll find suggested verses for you to memorize. These memory sections are marked by the word "Remember!" Whether or not you memorize these verses is up to you, but doing so would be a great way to intentionally hide God's word in your heart as you learn more about how to understand it.

- Chapters 2–7 each include a large section titled "Applying This Tool," where I show you how the tool we're examining in that chapter can be applied to selected passages of Scripture. In several places in each of these chapters, you'll be instructed to "Read!" a biblical passage. After each one, you'll find an explanation of how the tool for that chapter should be used to interpret that passage. These sections will make the most sense (and be most beneficial to you) if you take time to read the passages.
- At the end of each chapter, you'll find a quick recap of the chapter's main points. Then you'll see a "Pray!" section. This is an opportunity for you to talk to God about what you've just learned. I encourage you to make these prayer times a priority.

I hope that *Understanding God's Word* will help you do just what the title suggests—better understand the Bible—so that you can benefit from and live by its timeless truths.

Chapter 1

BASICS OF BIBLE STUDY

Bible study—and good interpretation and application of the Bible—can be difficult, to say the least. You've probably been involved in small-group Bible studies that have gone down various rabbit trails that seemed to have very little to do with the biblical text. And you've probably heard people make applications from Bible passages that made you ask yourself, "Is that *really* what this passage is about?" Even in your personal study of the Bible, there probably have been times when you've wondered, "How can I be sure that I'm understanding this passage in the right way so I can hear from God and rightly apply his word to my life?"

If you've ever been asked to teach the Bible, perhaps in a Sunday school or small-group context, you've probably felt the weight of some of these questions: Am I getting it *right*? Is *this* the main point of the text? Am I applying this passage *correctly* to God's people today? We want to be sure we're getting God's word right so that we can apply it faithfully to our lives as God intends.

All of these situations and struggles have to do with basic *biblical hermeneutics*—the process of understanding, interpreting, and applying the Bible. This book intends to give you some basic hermeneutical tools that you can put to use as you read the Bible on your own, study it in small groups, or perhaps even teach it in certain settings.

Each chapter in this book will introduce a different hermeneutical tool. All of these tools start with the letter *C* to make remembering them easier. I'll explain each tool, tell you what hermeneutical mistakes it helps you avoid and what benefits it provides, and then give several examples of how to use it in various passages of the Bible. I believe that if you use these tools faithfully and consistently, they will help you interpret the Bible accurately and apply it well.

The six tools that we'll learn about and apply are:

1. The *context* tool, which will help you notice and apply the historical, literary, and canonical context of the biblical passage you are studying.
2. The *courtroom* tool, which will remind you to commit to saying neither more nor less than what Scripture says.
3. The *crux* tool, by which you'll make sure that you are studying any given biblical passage in light of the main theme of the book in which its contained.
4. The *construction* tool, which will help you discern the structure and shape that the author has intentionally given to the passage.
5. The *clarity* tool, by which you'll seek to leave behind your personal perspectives and agendas, allowing the biblical text to speak for itself.
6. The *cross* tool, which will help you always study the Bible in light of its climax: the person and work of Jesus Christ, the Savior and Lord.

We'll begin unpacking these six tools in the next chapter. First, however, it will be helpful to consider several foundational principles about the Bible and think about some habits we need to develop in order to study it successfully.

FOUNDATIONAL PRINCIPLES

It's important to remember some of the theological principles about the Bible that give us confidence that we actually can study it, understand it, and apply it to our lives. After all, if the Bible is merely a human book, there is no ultimate reason to believe that it is *coherent* and *clear*, and that it can actually *change* us.

Is the Bible coherent? Scriptural coherence—in the Bible as a whole and even within each individual books—would be surprising if the Bible were nothing more than a human book. After all, the Bible was composed by more than forty human authors over hundreds of years. However, we can be confident about its coherence because of the doctrine of *inspiration* (see 2 Tim. 3:16). All Scripture, says the apostle Paul, is "breathed out" by God, who inspired the human authors to write exactly what he intended by the power and guidance of the Holy Spirit. As Christians, then, we understand that we study a book that was written by dozens of human authors but ultimately by one divine author. That means we can be confident that it is coherent and consistent in the story it tells, the truths it proclaims, the message it calls us to believe, and the responses it demands.

Is the Bible clear? To affirm that the Bible is clear is not to say that it has no difficult parts. Even the best and brightest scholars and pastors still debate—and disagree about—some passages of Scripture that are notoriously difficult to understand. But the doctrine of the Bible's clarity—or its *perspicuity*—reminds us that the central truths of Christianity are abundantly clear and understandable for everyone who reads it. There may be debate about the precise meaning of some passages or phrases, but the Bible does not leave us in doubt about who created the world, the sinfulness of man, the divinity of Christ, the need for repentance and faith, the substitutionary death of Jesus and his resurrection from the dead, and the reality of a coming final judgment. No one has to be a trained biblical scholar to understand these truths. One core conviction that underlies this book is that *ordinary Christians can study, understand, and apply God's word faithfully.* We believe this because the Bible, God's word, is clear.

Can the Bible change us? As I said just above, if the Bible is merely a human book, we have no reason to assume that it is either coherent or clear. We also have no reason to assume that Bible study—and teaching and preaching—should change us in any way. But the Christian conviction is that because the Bible is God's inspired word, it is *powerful.* The Bible doesn't just tell us about God—it is God's word, and that means it holds power to change, convict, transform, and build us up in Jesus Christ. Hebrews 4:12 reminds us that God's word is "living and active, sharper than any two-edged sword." In other words, it can "cut" us, wounding us with the painful yet healing truth of God, and call us to repentance and faith in Jesus. Christians should work to read, study, understand, and apply the Bible well because we really believe that God's word can change us. It is his way to accomplish his saving and sanctifying work in the lives and hearts of his people.

SIX HABITS FOR SUCCESSFUL BIBLE STUDY

As we conclude this chapter, let's consider Bible study—particularly Bible study that happens in a small-group setting. As I mentioned earlier, many of us have had the experience of sitting in a small-group Bible study that begins to go a bit off the rails in terms of the interpretations and applications offered by those in the group. We'll talk more about the way the hermeneutical tools that I discuss in this book can keep us on the rails in personal study, but I want to offer a plan for small-group Bible study that can help as well.

Years ago, when I was serving in high school ministry, we offered this simple plan to our students as they learned how to lead small-group Bible studies with their peers. It consists of the cultivation of six habits that constitute a basic approach to studying any passage of Scripture. Developing these habits will help keep you on track in your study—paying attention to the text, avoiding rabbit trails, and doing everything you can to get the main point and the central application as God intended it. Let's look at these habits.

Read carefully. Our first habit is simply careful reading. So many mistakes are made in hermeneutics (biblical interpretation) because people read too quickly through a passage, assume they understand what it's saying, and then make a leap to something in their experience that the passage makes them think about. Carefully reading the text several times can be the first and most important step in making sure we are listening to what the Bible is actually saying. Take time to read slowly. Make observations and linger over the text. Read it silently, then out loud. And don't forget to pray for God's help as you listen to his word and seek to understand and apply it faithfully.

Read in context. I'll say much more about this when we get to the context tool in chapter 2, but it's important to understand that mistakes in the interpretation and application of the Bible often can be avoided simply by taking time to understand the context of specific verses and passages. A verse that seems to be saying one thing at first glance could actually be understood to mean the opposite when it's read in its proper context. When we study the Bible, then, we need to pay attention to the verses directly around the passage we're reading. We need to think about the historical situation of the original audience in order to understand what the biblical author was saying to them before we apply the passage to ourselves. And we need to make sure that we are remembering the context of the entire Bible, which tells the story of God's creation, humanity's fall, redemption through Christ, and the promise of resurrected life in God's new creation. Reading every Bible passage—and every Bible verse—in its proper context is vital for proper understanding and application of God's word.

Identify core terms. Next, we must look for core words or phrases in a passage of Scripture. As we study a Bible passage, we must ask,

"What words or phrases are repeated? Are there ideas that keep coming up again and again in the passage? Is there a particular point that the author makes—perhaps at both the beginning and the end of a story or section of Scripture?" This habit is designed to help us get closer to the crux (main point) of the text (see the next habit) by identifying repeated emphases employed by the biblical author. When we tell a story or give a speech, we almost always repeat or emphasize the points that are most important to us. It's no different with the biblical text, so paying careful attention to repeated words often can be a helpful way to capture what God's word is saying to us.

Identify the main point. This habit can help pinpoint the theme of a passage of Scripture, which can be defined as the *timeless theological truth* that the passage is teaching. The theme of any biblical passage is just as true today as it was when the passage was written. It may be a truth about the character of God, humanity, sin, salvation, or our fallen world. Whatever it may be, an important discipline in Bible study is to work hard to capture that main point. Try to put this theme into just one sentence—something like "The main point of this passage is ________." Taking this step in Bible study doesn't mean you'll always get the main point exactly right, but it will help you discipline yourself to not only study a passage of Scripture verse by verse, but also to see a chunk of Scripture as a whole, seeking to discern the overall main point that the biblical author, as inspired by God the Holy Spirit, was making to his original audience (and is making to us, God's people today).

See Christ in the text. We'll spend a chapter later in this book considering faithful paths to the gospel that we can take in our study of any passage of Scripture (see chap. 7). The simple conviction behind this habit of Bible study is that the Scriptures ultimately are about God's redemption of sinners—and all of creation—through the life, death, resurrection, and final return of his Son, Jesus Christ. The Bible's climax is the saving work of God through Jesus Christ by the power of the Holy Spirit. So it's appropriate for us to ask, when studying any passage of Scripture, "How does this passage relate to Jesus and the gospel?" Of course, it's important to remember that different passages of Scripture point to Jesus and the gospel in different ways. Some Old Testament passages offer direct prophetic words about the coming of Jesus, while others simply display the need for Jesus, the Messiah, to come and save sinners. Some New Testament passages explain Jesus's work on the cross in detail; others apply his saving work or hold him out as an example for Christians to follow. Whatever the case may be, it's important—and valid—for Christians to seek to connect every passage in the Bible to the person and work of Jesus Christ, who is the Savior of all who believe.

Answer God's call. This is where the rubber meets the road. Here we ask that all-important question, "What does the truth of this passage mean for the way I think, act, and speak?" We are asking ourselves, "What is the central call of this passage to me as a follower of Jesus Christ?" We're talking, of course, about application. If the Bible is true—and if Jesus indeed is our Savior and Lord, who invites us to follow and obey him—then every passage of Scripture should have a real impact on our lives. If we do not practice this final habit of Bible study, there is a very real danger that while we may engage in some cerebral or academic study of Scripture, we will not allow the Bible to challenge and change us. God's word is living and active (Heb. 4:12); our Lord intends for us to obey it and to be constantly changed by it as it calls us to deeper obedience, sanctification, and growth in Christ. When we study the Bible, then, we are trying to discover what it *means*, but also what it means for the way we *live* as faithful followers of Jesus Christ.

These six habits can be extremely helpful as a basic plan for studying any passage of the Bible (on your own or in a small group of Christians—or non-Christians).

Now let's dive into learning the tools for biblical interpretation and application that make up the bulk of this book.

Chapter 2

THE CONTEXT TOOL

The first tool we'll learn about and then apply to the study of the biblical text is the *context* tool.

One quick initial note: while I will refer to what we're learning about as tools, a better word for them might be *principles*. They are big-picture principles that should guide and shape the way you approach every text in the Bible. When you put all of them together in your study of the biblical text, you will be much better equipped to interpret and apply the Bible in the way God intends. This is exciting because it means that God's word will then begin to work in the right ways in your life.

You do not need to have a seminary education to apply these tools or principles to your study of God's word. These are intended for use by ordinary Christians of all ages and from all walks of life. Any follower of Jesus who is willing to do some careful reading and intentional study of God's word can use them. My prayer is that, by the end of this book, you'll be able to put these tools in your metaphorical hermeneutical tool belt and be better equipped to study God's word, interpret it, apply it, and even teach it to others in the context of Bible studies, Sunday school classes, youth groups, and other gatherings. In other words, this book isn't for pastors, scholars, or seminarians—it's for you!

As I mentioned earlier, we will learn about six tools in this book and will practice putting them to work in many kinds of Bible passages. Hopefully they will become natural parts of the way that you approach and study God's word for the rest of your life.

Remember!

Jeremiah 29:11 is one of the passages on which you'll practice using the context tool later in this chapter. This is a wonderful promise from God to his people, so I encourage you to try to memorize it.

For I know the plans I have for you, declares the Lord, *plans for welfare and not for evil, to give you a future and a hope. (Jer. 29:11)*

UNDERSTANDING THIS TOOL

Have you ever said something that was taken out of context? If so, you know how frustrating that can be. Perhaps someone overheard you say something about a friend, and that someone caught only one phrase of the conversation—a phrase that made it sound as if you were saying something quite terrible about your friend. Perhaps when you were confronted about this, you said, "No! You are taking that phrase completely out of context. That's not what I meant at all!"

When you said that your words were taken out of context, you meant that although you *did* speak the actual words that were overheard, you spoke them in the context of a conversation—and if that conversation had been heard in its entirety, it would have been clear that you did *not* mean those words in the way the other person thought you meant them. If that person could only have heard the broader context, he would have *understood* and *interpreted* your words more accurately and truthfully.

Unfortunately, when we come to the Bible, we all too often do something very similar to what your friend did with your words: we take verses and passages from Scripture and rip them out of their proper context. Sadly, I believe that people tend to do this with the Bible even more than with other books that they read. Many times, people do this with good intentions. They are seeking to find a word of encouragement for their day, an inspiring quote for a friend, or a devotional thought to share with a small group, sports team, or business gathering. They read quickly, find a verse or verses that seem to work, and grab them and go, only to discover later that they wrongly interpreted verses by missing their broader context. Despite their good intentions, such disregard for context can often result in the abuse—and misuse—of the word of God.

Finding the right context of a Bible verse or passage is vitally important in order to make correct interpretation and application. When you apply the context tool, you will begin to see the way that it can guard and protect you against false interpretations of the Bible and lead you in both interpreting and applying God's word in the way that he intends.

Here is the principle behind the context tool:

> In our interpretation and application of any part of the Bible, we must make sure that we fully evaluate and comprehend every part of the context of the passage so that we can understand why the passage was written by the author and how it was understood by the original recipients. We will then be able to apply the text fully and faithfully to our lives.

To express this principle in a slightly different way, this tool reminds us that we must make the journey to the ancient world of the Bible in order to see every text in its context. Remember, when we study the Bible, we are digging into the living and inspired word of God, but it's an ancient text, written to people who lived and followed God thousands of years ago in contexts very different than ours. The Bible *does* have something to say to Christians today, of course—but we need to discover what the text meant *then* before we can rightly discern what it means for us *now*.

If we are studying the book of 1 Corinthians, for example, we must make the journey in our Bible study to the ancient city of first-century Corinth in order to see the issues and situation there. If we are studying the book of Genesis, then we need to travel to ancient Mesopotamia to see the situation of the early patriarchs of the faith. We should note the life situation of Paul as he writes his final letter to Timothy, and the situation of the persecuted church as Peter and John write their letters. Context matters! We need to take these kinds of journeys in order to get the meaning of the text right.

Here's a key point as we get ready to apply this first tool: *God's word can never mean something that it never meant!*

This is a wonderful way to summarize the context tool. We always need to work hard to see what God's word meant when it was written. Only then will we be able to see what it means for us as God's people today.

But what kinds of context do we need to be ready to evaluate as we apply this tool? As you'll see, reading and studying a biblical text in context means considering several factors.

Historical context. For every passage we study, we need to be aware of the historical context—both of the biblical author and of the original readers of the book. No biblical author wrote in a vacuum—all of them lived real lives in real places, and God used their experiences to help them communicate his word in the way that he intended. To get a feel for the historical context of a biblical passage, we have to ask some basic questions: When was this book written? Who was the original audience of this text? What was the political and cultural situation at the time of the writing? What was different for God's people then—and what is still the same for us today? It's not difficult to discover some basic details about the historical context of passages of Scripture—a good study Bible is a great place to start.

Literary context. Every word in the Bible is part of a sentence; every sentence is part of a wider paragraph or unit; and every paragraph or unit is part of an entire book. We must keep this in mind as we read and study the Bible, thinking about how verses and passages fit into books. To pay attention to the literary context means that we don't read the Bible like a collection of great quotations, from which we can pick and choose random inspirational sayings that mean whatever we want them to mean. The Bible is a literary work, coming to us in entire books within distinct literary genres: poetic writings, prophetic words, narratives (stories), epistles (letters), apocalyptic literature, and more. To pay attention to the literary context of every verse and passage in Scripture is to take seriously and respectfully the way God, in his perfect wisdom, has chosen to reveal his word to us.

Canonical context. Along with the verses, passages, and books of the Bible, we must think about the whole canon (the entire collection of books) of Scripture. Every book of the Bible is part of the one big story of God's saving work in the world, a story that is shown to us through all of Scripture. Faithful biblical scholars have agreed on a rule of thumb for studying difficult passages: *Scripture interprets Scripture.* That means that we always read any given part of the Bible in light of the rest of the Bible. We consider the entire scope of Scripture when we study any individual text—and we can do this because the entire Bible has one divine author. So when we think about the context of a passage in the Bible, we should ask ourselves, "Where does this passage fit in the overall arc of the biblical story? Where is it in God's plan for redemption?" If the Bible truly is one great unified story of his saving work in the world, these are important and legitimate questions for Bible study.

We'll soon begin putting this tool to work. It will prove to be very helpful as you study parts of the Bible. But first, let's consider some problems in Bible interpretation and application that can be avoided when the context tool is properly applied.

PROBLEMS AVOIDED WITH THIS TOOL

The context tool is not just a meaningless theory, but actually protects you from serious errors and abuses of God's word that can be damaging to both individual Christians and to the wider church.

Most problems with Bible interpretation originate from a motive that is not all bad: a desire for relevance. People want the Bible to have a relevant word for them—a teaching that will affect their lives and situation. They want God to speak powerfully right now. Unfortunately, this desire for immediate relevance often can lead people to ignore the issues of context and make verses of the Bible mean whatever they want them to mean.

Here are just a few problems that can result when this happens—problems that the context tool can help you avoid in your study:

False interpretation. Probably the most obvious problem that comes when context is completely ignored is false interpretation of a verse or passage of Scripture. Unfortunately, some passages of Scripture can be used to say the exact *opposite* of what they mean when people ignore context and read what they want into the verses. In the example passages that we will work through later in this chapter, we will see how this might happen. It is a travesty for biblical hermeneutics when, in a desire for relevance, a Bible verse is ripped from its context and interpreted to mean something that it never meant. This can mislead God's people and cause them to mistake a human voice for God's voice.

Missing the main point. A slightly less serious problem that can occur when context is not considered is that students of the Bible miss the main point of what a verse or passage is saying or teaching. Their interpretation may not be false or harmful, but it may not focus on the main point of the Bible verse or passage for God's people. In other words, they emphasize the wrong aspect or part of the passage by ignoring what should be emphasized given the context.

Abusing history. Sometimes when a person uses a verse or passage to say something that he or she wants it to say, his or her interpretation can be an abuse of history. To ignore the historical context of a passage in the Bible (the events, geographical location, characters, etc.) is to act as if the Bible somehow was not written in the context of the real history of the world. This is a very dangerous mindset in Bible study and interpretation because God's word has indeed broken powerfully into our world in the midst of real historical events. To ignore these events and read the Bible as if it has no relation to the historical context in which it was written is to misrepresent the real history of this world. The Bible *is* literature, but it speaks of real events that truly took place in the history of our world.

Ignoring inspiration. A slightly different slant on the above problem reveals another issue with ignoring the context of a passage in the Bible: doing so can lead to a denial of the way that our God inspired his word. He did it by guiding real human authors, through the work of his Holy Spirit, to write exactly what he wanted them to write. This means that there *is* a definite intended meaning in every text and passage of the Bible; the human authors really meant to make specific points. So our job as students of the Bible is to study each passage—and its context—very carefully in order to find our way to the intended meaning of the real human authors, who were inspired by God. To fail to study the Bible in this way is to treat it with less respect than we treat other great literature that we study with care and attention to detail.

BENEFITS RECEIVED WITH THIS TOOL

There are numerous benefits of putting the context tool to work effectively in Bible study, interpretation, and application. These benefits are important for Christians who are serious about hearing God's voice, as he really does speak to his people today through his inspired word. They include:

Finding the author's intended meaning. As I mentioned earlier, part of what it means to respect the historical context of the Bible—and the truth of inspiration itself—is to remember that real human authors really did write the words of Scripture for specific reasons at specific times. This means we need to look for their intended meaning in any given text of the Bible, and the context tool can help us find it.

God's inspiration of the Bible means that he is the ultimate author of Scripture; he spoke through human authors, whom he directed by his Holy Spirit, so that nothing in the Bible is there by accident. All of it is fully God's word, and everything is there exactly as he intended it to be. Even so, God chose to use real human authors to communicate his life-giving truth to the world. How did he do this? We must not confuse inspiration with dictation (the idea that God dictated, word by word, what the biblical authors were to write). God inspired the human authors of Scripture, but they wrote out of their own unique personalities, utilizing their human minds and writing in their own particular styles.

This means that it is possible and logical to talk about the author's intended meaning in any given text of the Bible. A passage does not mean whatever we want it to mean. It means what the original author, as directed by God's Holy Spirit, intended it to mean. A careful study of context can help us arrive at this meaning.

Hearing the passage as the original audience heard it. When we find our way to the intended meaning of the author, another very important thing happens: we begin to actually hear the passage as the original audience heard it. We hear a rebuke as a rebuke. We hear an encouragement as an encouragement. We begin to understand the specific situations, sins, or celebrations that God's people were experiencing when these words were written to them. It is important to gain this understanding, because only when we do so can we begin to apply a Bible passage faithfully to our lives. Only when we have heard a text as its original audience heard it can we know how we are to receive it now and how we should bring it to bear in a powerful way in the lives of God's people today.

Finding the real relevance of God's word. Earlier, we discussed the good intention that often leads people to wrong interpretations of the Bible—the desire for relevance as they read, interpret, and apply the Scriptures. People want to bring the Bible directly to their lives, so they try to make it apply to their situations without considering the real historical context of each passage or the intended meaning of the biblical authors. The sad reality is that, by doing this, people actually make God's word less relevant.

Think about this: What would be the most relevant truth that people who are created by God could hear? It would be the message of God speaking directly to them, as he does by his word. Considering the context of a passage, and working to get our interpretation and application right in light of that context, is actually the best way to relevantly read and study God's word in order to hear his voice clearly. There is nothing more relevant to the lives of people created by God than to hear from their Creator.

APPLYING THIS TOOL

Let's now put the context tool to work in the study of several Bible verses and passages. In each of these examples, you will begin by reading the verse or passage, then identify mistakes that people might make by failing to use the context tool, and end by seeking to interpret the verse or passage faithfully by putting the tool to work. The goal is to give you good practice in bringing context into your intentional study of every part of the Bible.

Jeremiah 29:11

Our first sample study will focus on a verse that probably is quite familiar to you.

READ!

Read Jeremiah 29:1–14 carefully and thoughtfully, noting the context in which verse 11 is contained. Take note of what you see there and think about how it might have an impact on the way you would interpret this verse and apply it to your life today.

How would ignoring the context of this verse in Jeremiah impact how we interpret and apply it?

The verse declares that God has "plans" for his people, and these plans are good. They are plans "for welfare and not for evil," plans to give them a "future" and a "hope." For many people, the tendency is to go from this verse directly to a great and general promise from God to his people in every age. Looking only at this verse, the promise seems to be one of blessing, wealth, success, and a bright future for all who follow God. Taken to an extreme, a verse like this can even be understood as a promise that God will shower his people with material blessings and that life will go well for them no matter what.

So ripped from its context, Jeremiah 29:11 could be taken as a promise that God has only good things for us on earth: prosperity, success, and health.

However, you know—probably from your own life—that prosperity, health, and success are not always the experience of God's faithful people. What, then, should we do with this verse in Jeremiah that seems to promise those things—at least on a first reading?

Let's begin by thinking about the *historical* context of this verse. God's people, according to Jeremiah 29:1, are in exile in Babylon. Their country has been conquered, their city has been destroyed, and they are slaves in a foreign land. Their situation is not good. So whatever Jeremiah is promising to God's people, it cannot be that bad things will never happen to them. A very bad thing has *already* happened to them: exile.

Next, let's consider the *literary* context. By reading verse 10—just one verse before verse 11—we see that God promises his people that they will be exiles in Babylon for seventy years! So whatever verse 11 means, it is not saying that God's people will never have to deal with difficult situations and circumstances. In fact, they may have long periods of suffering. This promise is pointing to future blessings that will come to God's people after a seventy-year stay in Babylon.

Finally, let's think about the *canonical* context of the Bible. We know from many other parts of the Bible that while some of God's people experience material blessing and peaceful lives, many do not. Some suffer and are persecuted for their faith, and others are even put to death because of their belief in Jesus Christ. Think about David (in the wilderness years), Job, Jeremiah, and the apostle Paul. Jesus himself saved God's people by *suffering and dying* on a cross for their sins. So the canonical context reminds us that verse 11 cannot be a promise that life will always be easy and full of material blessing for God's people. God's people often face pain, trouble, and suffering.

When we put all of this together, we begin to understand what verse 11 is saying to God's people in its context. It is not a promise of immediate material prosperity or that their lives will be easy all the time; after all, God's people were in exile for seventy years. But it is a promise that God really has a long-term, eternal plan for the good of those who are his. All of God's people really have a future and a hope through Jesus Christ. There may be suffering and hardship first. Ultimately, though, God's eternal plan for his true people is a good one. He is a faithful and loving God who brought his people back to the promised land after seventy years and promises to bring all his faithful people to their eternal home with him in the new heaven and new earth.

Philippians 4:13

Let's turn now to another very well-known verse that can easily be ripped from its context. You may have seen it on the walls of a Christian gym or weight room; you may have even heard it used to motivate you as you played a sport or got ready to take a test or run a race. Sadly, it is often misused in these and similar ways because its context is ignored.

READ!

Read Philippians 4:13 (without reading the surrounding verses yet). Think about some conclusions you might draw about what this verse is saying if you ignore the context.

In this verse, Paul is saying that he can do "all things" through Christ, who strengthens him. As I suggested above, you probably have seen this verse used in the context of athletics or some other kind of competition. Some people have even made it their "life verse" as they think about Jesus helping them do amazing things. In other words, when we totally ignore the context that surrounds this verse, it becomes all about accomplishment. We can take it as a promise that Jesus will strengthen us to do the things that we want to do—win a game, pass a test, make a lot of money, or achieve a great award. We can be tempted to use this verse as a kind of motivational slogan for our lives.

But when we look at the context, putting the tool we're learning about in this chapter to work, we begin to see that we cannot really take this verse as being about our achievements.

First, let's consider the *historical* context. With just a quick bit of reading in the book of Philippians, we find that Paul is writing this letter from prison—probably in Rome (see chap. 1 of the book). This means that, for Paul, this verse is certainly not talking about accomplishment, because he is not accomplishing much of anything—at least not humanly speaking. He is chained up in prison, dependent on his friends for food and other provisions, and seemingly not doing "all things" that he might want to do if he were a free man.

Next, let's think about the *literary* context. When we read Philippians 4:10–12, we see that Paul is in the midst of a discussion about *contentment*, not accomplishment. He is talking about the way that God has helped him remain content whether he has a lot or a little, is hungry or full, is suffering or doing well, or is abounding or sitting in poverty. So the literary context shows us that doing "all things" does not refer only to times of blessing, celebration, and victory. It refers to the power—the "secret" (v. 12)—of remaining content in Christ in every changing circumstance.

Finally, let's consider the *canonical* context of this verse. We know from the rest of Scripture that Christ does accomplish amazing things in and through his people, but it is always for his glorious gospel purposes. Only rarely is it about their accomplishments, and it is never ultimately about their earthly glory or fame. The whole Bible reminds us that God strengthens his people for his purposes, not theirs. Not only that, God is honored through the faithful suffering of his people, just as he is through their successes and accomplishments.

So when we look at the whole picture of the context of Philippians 4:13, we begin to see that Paul is not talking about accomplishment but about contentment. He is saying that Jesus Christ can strengthen him to be content, joyful, and at peace in every situation of life—even the difficult ones. This is how God wants to speak to us today from this passage. He wants to remind us that Jesus really is enough—enough to strengthen us to be content in him no matter what we are facing. That's Paul's "secret"—and it should be ours also as we find in Jesus our unchanging treasure and joy amid ever-changing circumstances.

Revelation 3:20

Turning to another well-known verse, we will see how our understanding of the context in which it occurs impacts its *tone*, which often causes it to be interpreted and applied incorrectly.

READ!

Read Revelation 3:20 (don't read the surrounding verses yet). What might we conclude about Jesus's general tone just by reading this verse? To whom might we imagine that Jesus is saying these words?

Considered on its own, Revelation 3:20 seems to be a very pleasant invitation from Jesus. His tone seems gentle, kind, and inviting, and the audience that he is addressing seems to be unbelievers, whom he is inviting to come into fellowship with him. You can imagine this verse being used to encourage people who do not know Jesus to open themselves to him as he knocks gently and patiently at the doors of their hearts. It seems that verse 20 might be a wonderful model for evangelism—or even to use directly in an evangelistic message or conversation.

The picture of Jesus knocking gently and issuing an invitation into a personal relationship with him is indeed a beautiful one. And it is true that Jesus often is described in Scripture as welcoming sinners into fellowship with him if they will repent and put their faith in him. But when we look at the context of this particular verse, we see that Jesus's tone is not what it initially seems to be, and unbelievers are not his intended audience.

Let's think first about the *historical* context. This one will take a bit more research than the other verses we've examined with the context tool so far, but as I noted above, you can find this basic information in a good study Bible. Laodicea, the home of the church to which this section of Revelation 3 is addressed, was an ancient city that was known for its putrid water supply. Because water had to be piped from other cities using long aqueducts, it came in as "neither hot nor cold" but "lukewarm" (v. 16), so it was disgusting to drink (it probably was dirty from the pipes and warm from the hot sun). In this passage, Jesus is comparing Laodicea to its water, saying that the people there—like their water—are so disgusting, they make him want to throw up! That certainly changes the tone of this verse we're considering.

Next, let's consider the *literary* context. In the verses that lead up to verse 20, Jesus is sternly rebuking the people of the church at Laodicea for their lack of humility and dependence on him. They think that they are "rich," not realizing that they are actually "wretched, pitiable, poor, blind, and naked" (v. 17). Probably this church had prospered greatly and had begun to forget its need for the grace of Jesus Christ. The problem is a deep sense of spiritual pride and self-sufficiency, which is a very dangerous sin. So it does not make sense to take verse 20 as a gentle and mild invitation to unbelievers to come into fellowship with Jesus. This is not an evangelistic verse; this is a stern rebuke and warning from Jesus to a church that is in danger of forgetting its deep need for him. It's intended for backslidden, proud believers who need to be called to repentance.

Finally, let's think about the *canonical* context. We have already mentioned that there are many passages in the Bible that show Jesus as a gentle and kind Savior who invites people into fellowship with God by grace. So to interpret verse 20 in this way is not to go against the teaching of the Bible. But it is to miss the point of this specific passage in its context. When we consider that context, we see an important rebuke from Jesus, who is obviously disgusted with a church full of believers who have come to think that they can do everything on their own, without help from the one who is the only Lord and Savior of lost and poor sinners. To take this verse otherwise is to make the mistake of teaching the *right* thing from the *wrong* text. We need to carefully allow every passage of Scripture to speak for itself, as God intended.

1 Corinthians 13

First Corinthians 13 is another passage in which the tone is often misunderstood and misrepresented. This passage is often referred to as the "love chapter" of Paul's letter to the Corinthian church because of its beautiful focus. However, the tone of this passage—and its function within the letter—is often misrepresented to students of the Bible when the wider context of the letter is not considered.

READ!

Read 1 Corinthians 13:1–7. What seems to be the tone? Where have you heard this passage used, read, or applied? Consider some of the ways people might hear these verses. Why might even many unbelievers enjoy reading and thinking about this passage?

If we were to take this chapter on its own and ignore the wider context of Paul's first letter to the church at Corinth, we might see it as a random poem about the beauty of love. "Love is patient and kind," writes Paul (1 Cor. 13:4). "Love never ends" (v. 8). We might imagine these words being read out in a sweet voice at a wedding (and, indeed, this chapter has been read at many weddings). We might be tempted to see it as simply a beautiful explanation of what love looks like.

Yet when we see this chapter in this way, we have become guilty of ripping it from its context in the wider letter and failing to see the power and emotion that is behind this chapter as it was written by Paul. It's not a freestanding love poem; it's part of a letter written by one of the apostles to an ancient church.

So how should we put our context tool to work in this passage?

First, let's consider the *historical* context. We know that Paul is writing to a church in the ancient city of Corinth, which was infamous for its sinful perversion, partying, and wild living. We know, too, that this church is gifted but immature; the people are actually *not* loving one another well at all. Instead, they are suing one another, fighting with one another, and even using the Lord's Supper as an excuse to make more divisions between the rich and poor people in the congregation (see chaps. 3, 6, and 11). This is the real context in which Paul is writing this letter; this is not a very loving church despite all of its spiritual gifts.

Next, let's think about the *literary* context. Paul uses many words in this short love chapter that he has used earlier in the book. In other words, this poem does not come out of nowhere. It is tied in with the rest of his letter to the Corinthians, which is largely a letter of *rebuke*. For example, Paul says in this chapter that love is not "arrogant" (1 Cor. 13:4). Just a few chapters earlier, Paul called out the Corinthians for being "arrogant" about sexual sin that was going on in their congregation (5:2). Paul says that love does not "insist on its own way" (13:5) after earlier rebuking the Corinthian believers for the divisive factions at play in the church body (1:10–17; 3:1–9). He says that love "bears all things" (13:7) rather than dragging other believers into court (6:1–11).

In other words, this chapter, especially given Paul's reference to other parts of the letter, is a continuation of the same tone of stern rebuke. Paul is saying that love is one thing and the Corinthians are exactly the opposite. For example, love is not arrogant but they are arrogant (even about perverse sexual sin in their midst).

Finally, let's consider the *canonical* context. While a random poem about love is certainly not unbiblical, many of the letters of the New Testament are written to address problems in the early church of Jesus Christ. There are other letters that address a lack of grace, forgiveness, and love among the believers in early congregations. So as Paul rebukes the Corinthians in this chapter for their lack of love by showing them a picture of what real love should look like, he is in line with much of the teaching of the New Testament. The apostle is holding up a portrait of Christlike love and rebuking the Corinthian church for failing miserably to live up to it. He is calling these Christians to repent—and to change.

Genesis 39

For one last example of the use of the context tool, we are going to go way back in the Scriptures to the book of Genesis to another fairly well-known passage. It is the account of Joseph and the wife of Potiphar, who develops quite an attraction to Joseph. Joseph, as you may remember, has been sold by his brothers (the sons of Jacob) into slavery and has ended up in the house of Potiphar, the captain of the guard in Egypt. Genesis 39 picks up the account of Joseph as he serves faithfully in the house of this army commander. Our goal is to see this passage in its right context in the flow of the story of Genesis in order to understand what the author of Genesis is emphasizing.

READ!

Read Genesis 39. Think about some of the main applications you've encountered as you've studied or heard preaching on this passage. Then glance back at Genesis 38. What do you notice about the setting of that chapter? What is surprising about the placement—and setting, characters, etc.—of that chapter given the content of Genesis 37 and Genesis 39?

What is the emphasis in the application of Genesis 39 when it is read without considering the wider context of the story of Genesis? It is seen as being all about fleeing sexual temptation. We see Joseph constantly bombarded by the sexual advances of Potiphar's wife (whom we can only assume is a beautiful woman, although the text does not say). We note his resistance to her attacks day after day. In the climactic moment of the story, Joseph actually runs away from Potiphar's wife, leaving his cloak behind him (v. 12). This portion of the story has often been used as a graphic illustration of the way that we, as believers, should run away from sin—a good reminder for all of us. We are to flee temptation, and especially sexual temptation.

This emphasis is not a bad one; it is certainly there in the text. But it is not the main focus of the author.

You glanced back at Genesis 38 a moment ago. Strangely, that chapter takes you back to the land of Canaan. Chapter 37 ends with Joseph in Egypt, and chapter 39 begins again with Joseph in Egypt. Why does the author give us a flashback to Joseph's brother Judah in Canaan in chapter 38 when the story seems to have shifted to Joseph in Egypt? That's a lot of jumping around—and it must be intentional on the part of the narrator.

When we consider the *literary* context of what is happening in Genesis, we begin to understand what the author is doing. In chapter 38, we see a man—Judah—and a woman—Tamar. In chapter 39, we also see a man—Joseph—and a woman—Potiphar's wife. Judah is a free man in the land of Canaan; Joseph is a slave in the land of Egypt. The author of Genesis is intentionally placing these two men side by side to show us a contrast. Judah does something terrible: he has a sinful sexual relationship with his daughter-in-law, and then tries to put her to death because of it. Judah is free, but he is a slave to sin. Joseph, an actual slave, stands strong against sin. Even though he is in chains, he is free in his obedience to God. In fact, as chapter 39 ends, we see that the Lord is with Joseph even in prison, where he is placed after the false accusation of Potiphar's wife (v. 23).

We will not discuss the historical and canonical context here because it is the literary context—the context of the wider story of Genesis—that is really most important at this point. Do you see how the author of Genesis is weaving together the story of Joseph with the story of Judah, his brother back in Canaan? Do you see that, while the importance of fleeing sexual temptation is certainly part of the application of this section of Genesis, it is not the main focus? The author of Genesis is showing how Joseph, though a slave, is still living under the blessing of God in the land of Egypt while his brother is living as a slave to sin back home.

This example also shows us the importance of considering larger chunks of Scripture all together, particularly as we study and apply Old Testament narratives. We often can't see what the author is doing unless we take a step back and see the big picture of how he is telling the story.

REVIEW

This chapter has introduced you to the first of six tools for your study of the Bible—the context tool. This tool helps you understand a passage as the author meant it to be read and as the original audience actually read it. You learned about three main kinds of context: historical, literary, and canonical. Finally, you put this tool to work as you looked at several passages of Scripture in which the context helps determine the meaning. In the next few chapters, we will learn about several more important tools and also spend time thinking about how to use them in actual verses and passages from the Bible.

PRAY!

As you close this chapter on the context tool, spend a few minutes talking to God about all that you have learned. Pray that he would help you apply this tool to your study of his word. Ask him to help you do this not just to gain "head knowledge" about Scripture, but in order to really hear his voice speaking to you through his inspired word.

Chapter 3

THE COURTROOM TOOL

In every American courtroom, a witness who takes the stand during a trial is asked to answer this question: "Do you swear to tell the truth, the whole truth, and nothing but the truth?" When that question is answered affirmatively, the witness can then be examined and the trial can continue.

That commitment—telling the truth, the whole truth, and nothing but the truth—is really the main idea behind the hermeneutical tool that we are going to learn about and then put to work in this chapter. When it comes to interpreting and applying the Bible, we are called as Christians to give "the whole truth" of God's word—and nothing but that truth! This is why I have chosen to call the tool for this chapter the *courtroom* tool. Our first task will be to gain an understanding of the principle that lies behind it.

Many people, of course, do not use the courtroom tool in their interpretation and application of the Bible. Unfortunately, ignoring this tool can lead to all kinds of problems in biblical interpretation, and we will talk about some of them. However, we'll also look at the rich benefits that come to us when we use this tool wisely. We'll conclude by applying it to several actual biblical texts.

Remember!

Your suggested memory verses for this chapter come from Deuteronomy 5—and they reflect the humble heart that God's people must have toward his word as they seek to follow it without turning aside in any direction—that is, without saying more or less than it says.

You shall be careful therefore to do as the LORD your God has commanded you. You shall not turn aside to the right hand or to the left. You shall walk in all the way that the LORD your God has commanded you, that you may live, and that it may go well with you, and that you may live long in the land that you shall possess. (Deut. 5:32–33)

UNDERSTANDING THIS TOOL

We can state the principle that lies behind the courtroom tool in this way:

> As we study the Bible and apply it to our lives, our goal is to say *neither more nor less* than what the Bible itself says.

The goal in Bible study, in other words, is to stay exactly on the "line" of Scripture—to go neither above it nor beneath it. Many people try to make the Bible say more than what it actually says; we will talk about the problems that this causes just below. Other people try to make the Bible say less than what it actually says; we will also talk about the serious problems—in both interpretation and in application to the Christian life—that this can cause. Christians who study the Bible faithfully are trying to get at the clear, true word of God—the truth, the whole truth, and nothing but the truth. They know that this is what will be best for their lives and hearts.

The only way to get to this point is through careful study of Scripture as we take it at face value. We need to read the Bible carefully—and we need to do our best to leave our opinions and preconceptions at the door when we come to Bible study. We also need to approach God's word with an attitude of humility, coming ready to hear his word in all of its power, purity, and challenge. This is not easy to do because sometimes the Bible makes us uncomfortable—especially if it is putting a finger on sin in our lives.

For Christians who really want to follow Jesus and hear God's word, this tool is incredibly important and useful. It serves as a constant reminder for us to receive God's word as it really is. Careful and faithful students of the Bible commit to reading and studying it without adding to it or subtracting from it.

PROBLEMS AVOIDED WITH THIS TOOL

I noted above that many people are tempted to say either more or less than what the Bible actually says. Now we are going to look in more detail at the serious problems that result from a failure to apply the courtroom tool to the study of the Bible. As we will see, the danger with trying to say either more or less than what the Bible itself says is that it can lead to much more than slightly misguided teaching; it actually can lead to sinful lifestyles and behaviors.

First, what are some problems that might result from people saying and applying *more* than what the Bible teaches? By adding things to God's word, they fail to hold to the "nothing but the truth" aspect of the principle that lies behind our tool for this chapter. That can lead to *legalism* or *spiritual pride*.

Legalism. When this mistake is made, people can fall into the trap of legalism. Legalism is the practice of adding rules, commands, and obligations to the Christian life that are not found in the Bible. People who make this mistake often even teach that these legalistic rules are a way to earn favor with God. The sad result is that people who make this mistake are often plagued by guilt (because they cannot live up to their own legalistic standards) and often place unnecessary guilt on others by calling them to hold to beliefs or practices that are actually not part of God's word. Legalism is a sad, antigospel approach to Christian living.

Spiritual pride. Another problem that might result from saying more than what God's word teaches is a kind of attitude of superiority or spiritual pride. From the perspective of people who add commands and teachings to God's word, those who do not add those same commands can seem to be not quite as holy or committed as they are. This can lead them to a (completely unfounded) sense of superiority that causes them to begin to look down on the people around them for not following their extra practices and commands. Such an attitude can fuel a dangerous spiritual pride and arrogance that leads to a lack of humility, a trait that is required of every follower of Jesus Christ.

Next, what are some problems that might result from a desire to say *less* than what the Bible teaches? Two major dangers are *liberalism* and *license*.

Liberalism. People who try to say less than what the Bible teaches can often fall into the trap of liberalism. By *liberalism*, I mean simply the practice of being liberal—or overly free—with the use and application of God's word. People begin to make the Bible say less than what it actually says by making excuses for why it cannot possibly mean what it seems to mean. (We will look at some examples later in this unit of how this can happen with specific parts of Scripture.) Such a "loose" approach to the Bible is very dangerous. It usually is driven by an attempt to water down some of the more difficult passages of Scripture or those that seem offensive to our cultural sensibilities today. Quite often, the motivation is to help Scripture match up with certain behaviors or lifestyles that people desire to accept or affirm. The dangerous result is that the clear teaching of Scripture is bent, twisted, or completely ignored.

License. Another problem with saying less than what the Bible says is license. By *license*, I mean a sense of freedom to live in whatever way we want to live—however sinful that may be. If a tendency toward legalism seeks to place additional laws, rules, and regulations on people by adding to God's word, license seeks to release people from the calls and commands that the Bible really does teach. The result can be terrible sin that can separate people from a relationship with Jesus.

BENEFITS RECEIVED WITH THIS TOOL

Just as there are problems with neglecting the courtroom tool, there is a positive side to using it. Several benefits come to us when we faithfully and carefully receive and apply God's word in all of its truth, beauty, and power. They include *balanced interpretation* and *protection from ourselves.*

Balanced interpretation. A commitment to using this tool in the study of the Bible will lead to balanced interpretation and application. In other words, it will help a Christian resist the urge to fall off the line of Scripture into either legalism or liberalism.

When we commit ourselves to really studying, interpreting, and applying the Bible as it comes to us, we see that Scripture is quite balanced; it asks us to hold many different teachings and truths with a kind of tension. For example, the Bible calls us to diligent obedience and holiness—something that people who are legalistic enjoy emphasizing and teaching about. But the Bible also reveals the incredible, full, and rich grace of God, which saves sinners through the cross of Jesus Christ, not through anything that they can do. Those truths—a call to obedience and the fullness of God's grace to save sinners—are held together with perfect joyful tension in Scripture.

The courtroom tool reminds us not to emphasize one more than the other, but to always stay on the line of the Scripture passage that we are studying, teaching, or applying. Believers in Jesus are saved fully by God's grace, but they are called to strive toward holiness.

Protection from ourselves. The courtroom tool also can protect us from allowing our own personal agendas, viewpoints, and backgrounds to dominate the way that we receive and interpret the Bible. We all have these agendas and viewpoints. We all bring different cultural backgrounds and presuppositions to the table when we come to God's word. But the courtroom tool reminds us that we all—regardless of our viewpoints and backgrounds—need to sit at the feet of God as he teaches us through his word. We all need to commit to hearing the truth, the whole truth, and nothing but the truth of the Bible. This is a word that transcends culture, and we need to be faithful to let it be the rule and guide for our lives. We don't add to it or subtract from it. We submit to it.

When used well, the courtroom tool is a key principle that can help us work toward humbly hearing God's true voice in Scripture rather than following our own desires to make the Bible say what we might like it to say.

APPLYING THIS TOOL

In this section, we're going to put the courtroom tool to work in the study of several Bible passages. First, however, let's look at two passages that illustrate one of the problems I mentioned above: legalism.

Genesis 3:1–7

We see a clear example of how the courtroom tool was ignored by two individuals in the very first pages of the Bible. The account of the fall in Genesis 3 is sad, yet it serves as a wonderful illustration of the importance of the courtroom tool in our interaction with God's word—and of the devastating danger of failing to put it to work.

READ!

Read Genesis 3:1–7. Consider some ways that Eve and Satan (the serpent) fail to apply the courtroom tool to their interaction with the word of God. Think about how God's word is used, abused, and even denied in these verses, and how these approaches to God's clear commands might serve as a warning to us as students of the Bible.

As we look at Genesis 3 in relation to the courtroom tool, we are going to essentially answer three simple questions:

- How does Eve fail to speak "nothing but the truth" of God's word in this passage?
- How does the serpent fail to speak "the whole truth" about God's word in this passage?
- What is the terrible result of the way that God's word is abused in this account?

We are going to see, in the earliest pages of Scripture, the importance of clearly seeing, hearing, and receiving the truth of God's word demonstrated for us.

So how does Eve fail to speak nothing but the truth of God's word in this passage? Remember what God commanded Adam and Eve in Genesis 2:16–17. He had given them nearly every tree in the garden of Eden for food—they were forbidden to eat from only one tree. That was it; that was the entire command—the full word—of the good God who had created Adam and Eve.

What does Eve do as she talks with the serpent? She *adds* to God's word. She says that not only must they not "eat" from this one tree, but they are not allowed to even "touch" it (Gen. 3:3). What is Eve doing here? She is actually becoming the first *legalist*. She is adding commands to God's word that God never gave to his people. She is failing to speak God's truth and nothing but God's truth. This is dangerous because, in adding to God's word, Eve is misrepresenting God and making him seem stricter than he actually is.

Satan, the serpent, very intentionally does exactly the opposite. He says *less* than what God's word says. "You will not surely die," he tells Eve (Gen. 3:4), completely denying the reality of God's judgment and justice to punish sin and rebellion against his word. It is interesting that the first word of God that Satan denies in this world is the word about *judgment*—the very real and very serious consequences for sin. He wants Adam and Eve to believe that there will not really be any serious punishment if they disobey God. He subtracts from God's word—and denies its truth completely.

Adam, sadly, is right there with Eve in her failure to rightly apply God's word. The text says that he is "with" her as she has this conversation with Satan (Gen. 3:6). Adam fails to hold the line of God's word as well. He could speak up. He could call Eve to state the whole truth and nothing but the truth of God's word. But he does not. He believes Satan, too, and he eats the fruit that God had told them not to eat. The consequence for this, of course, is the great fall of mankind. Sin enters the world because human beings fail to live under the good word of the Creator God.

Can you see how this first great "battle" in the garden of Eden was over the right response to the word of God? Do you see how important it is for us today to hold to the simple and clear truth of the Bible—refusing to add to it or subtract from it? This sad day for God's people reminds us of the importance of holding on, to the best of our ability, to the whole truth—and nothing but the truth—of the word of our God and Savior.

Mark 7:1–13

In our next passage, you are going to learn about some legalists during Jesus's day—the Pharisees. Like Eve, they chose to *add* things to God's word, saying *more* than what God had said. As you will see, Jesus did not have a very positive response to these people and their failure to apply the courtroom tool. We will identify where they went wrong and how we can avoid falling into the same legalistic trap.

READ!

Read Mark 7:1–13. Think about the way the Pharisees are obviously saying more than what God's word says. Consider Jesus's response—and what he says they have unwittingly done with the word of God (even though they are trying to be very holy and religious).

As the scene opens in Mark 7, we see the Pharisees getting upset with Jesus's disciples for not washing their hands before they eat. Is this something that is specifically against God's word? No! In fact, the passage tells us that this ritual of handwashing is "holding to the tradition of the elders" (v. 3). In other words, this is not part of the law of Moses, but is a tradition that the Pharisees' forefathers created in addition to God's law. So the Pharisees clearly are guilty of saying *more* than what God's word says. They have added extra rules to Scripture based on their human traditions.

Jesus calls them out on this, telling them that, through all their additions of laws, they have failed to have true hearts of worship to God. Their hearts are actually "far" from God (v. 6). This is a devastating rebuke to these Pharisees, who think of themselves as very religious.

Jesus then goes on to identify another area in the Pharisees' lives and teaching where they have said *more* than God's word and failed to speak nothing but the truth about what God says. Moses's law commands God's people to "honor" their fathers and mothers (v. 10). But the Pharisees have added a special exception to this rule. People doing ministry or special work for God can ignore the obligation to take care of their parents because they are giving a gift ("Corban," v. 11) to God with their lives. So many of them, since they think of themselves as in service to God (a much more holy calling than caring for aging parents), feel that they can neglect the care and honor of their parents.

Jesus says that this is terrible. He goes on to explain to the Pharisees that this "tradition" (v. 13), in which they think they are being quite holy, is actually making the word of God "void," or meaningless. The Pharisees are trying to say even *more* than God's word says, so they are failing to obey the very word that they claim to value. By trying to *add* to God's word, they end up *subtracting* from it.

So here, according to Jesus, is the danger of legalism: the system of extra rules that people use to try to make themselves more religious and holy ends up saying less than what God's word says. People are trying to be better than those around them who hold to the simple truth of the Bible—but they end up being much worse.

Matthew 5:27–30

Having seen some of the negative consequences of adding to God's word, let's now put the courtroom tool to work in the study of several other Bible passages. Just as you did in the previous chapter when you studied the context tool, you're going to read several passages, then identify the mistakes that people might make by failing to use the courtroom tool in their study of those portions of Scripture, and finally seek to interpret the passages faithfully by putting the tool to work.

First, we will use the tool as we study Jesus's words about the Christian response to the sin of lust and adultery in Matthew 5. Our goal is to see how people might try to say either more or less about this text than what God's word says, then move to the right application of this passage, which says nothing but the truth about this word from God.

READ!

Read Matthew 5:27–30. Think about how we might be tempted to say more or less than what God's word says in this passage.

If someone wanted to say more than this passage is teaching, they might take these words of Jesus extremely literally. One could teach, for example, that a person should literally do damage to his or her body in response to sin. After all, the passage talks about tearing out eyes and cutting off hands. So to say more than the truth of this passage might be to tell people that, when they sin, they need to hurt themselves in some way in order to stop sinning. There have been examples throughout church history of people who applied this passage in extremely literal (and gruesome) ways.

Conversely, how might someone try to say less than what this passage is teaching? They might try to make this passage so metaphorical (just using word pictures in a nonliteral way) that it really does not mean anything at all. In other words, a person might say that since Jesus could not possibly be telling people to cut off their hands, this passage is just a picture that we do not need to take very seriously. According to this interpretation, the passage does not really have any power in our lives; Jesus is using exaggerated language to make a point, so we can dismiss any literal application of his words.

How do we speak the whole truth—and nothing but the truth—from this passage into our lives as followers of Jesus? How do we avoid saying more or less than what this passage teaches?

First of all, Jesus is not being completely literal about tearing out eyes and cutting off hands. For Jesus to command the literal removal of body parts would be a denial of the goodness of God's creation and a direct contradiction of his care for human beings in both their souls and bodies. Still, Jesus is being incredibly and violently serious about our response to sin in our lives. According to his definition of adultery (simply lusting in the heart), we all are guilty of this sin before God, so we all need to be saved by his grace to us in Christ. So as we come to Jesus as our Savior, we are to commit to a violent putting away of the sin for which he died. We are to "tear . . . out" and "cut . . . off" (Matt. 5:29–30) things in our lives that distract us from Jesus and lead us into temptation—whether that be internet sites, magazines, or harmful relationships. Jesus is calling for an all-out war against sin as we follow him in obedience and the pursuit of sexual purity and holiness.

This approach to this passage brings us close to finding the true principle that we need to apply; it avoids an overly literal application, but also avoids saying less than what the passage says, so that it becomes meaningless. We may not cut off a literal hand, but we may throw away a phone, delete an app, or stop watching certain shows or listening to certain music.

1 John 1:5–10

Our next passage calls for especially balanced interpretation and application. It would be very easy to fall off to the right or the left as we study 1 John 1:5–10. Our goal is to use the courtroom tool to see the whole truth and nothing but the truth from this important part of the Bible.

READ!

Read 1 John 1:5–10. Think about some ways that we might say more than what this passage is teaching and ways that we might be tempted to water it down by saying less than what it says. What might lead us to a balanced interpretation, one that holds on to the biblical tension that we find in this passage?

We are going to think through two very extreme views on 1 John 1:5–10, each one focusing on particular verses but not taking into account the whole truth of this passage. In a way, one of these views tries to say more than what the passage is saying, while the other one tries to say less than what the passage teaches. Both of these mistakes come from overemphasis on one side of a tension that the Bible holds perfectly, consistently, and clearly.

First, think about an interpretation and application from 1 John 1:5–10 that primarily focuses on verses 5–7. What is the focus there? It is on the call to Christians to "walk in the light" (v. 7)—in other words, to not walk in the "darkness" of sin (v. 6), but to follow Jesus in obedience and holiness. The passage rightly points out that a claim of fellowship with Jesus that is not backed up by a life of obedience to him must be a lie.

But with an extreme interpretation of these verses, a person might claim that Christians must be completely perfect—sinless in some way. They might read these verses as saying that if a Christian commits a sin, he or she must not really know Jesus at all. A claim of sinless perfection could come from these verses, as well as a belief in the possibility of total sanctification for followers of Jesus in this life. That is saying more than what this text is saying, as we will see in a moment.

Second, think about an interpretation and application from 1 John 1:5–10 that primarily focuses on verses 8–10. Those verses address the need to be honest about our sins so that we can confess them and find God faithful to forgive us for them through the cleansing blood of Jesus. To claim that we have "not sinned" is actually to call God a liar (v. 10).

Yet if we focus only on these verses, we might ignore verses 5–7 and take sin in the Christian life too lightly—after all, we have sinned and have been forgiven. Someone might be tempted to ask, "Is it OK if I keep on sinning as long as I am honest about it and keep asking for forgiveness? After all, everybody does it!" That is saying less than what this whole passage is saying.

So how do we speak the truth, the whole truth, and nothing but the truth from this passage? How do we avoid saying more or less than what this passage is teaching?

We must affirm both the need for believers to pursue holiness and stop sinning, as well as the reality of sin that constantly demands confession and a return to the gracious God who gave his Son to die for sins. In other words, we must make sure that we focus equally on verses 5–7 and 8–10.

As I noted above, this passage contains a tension that God's word asks us to hold in our hearts, lives, and biblical interpretation. It is the tension between the free grace that saves us and the drive for obedience and holiness that is to characterize our lives as followers of Jesus who have been justified freely by his grace through faith. We must emphasize both of these things in order to avoid saying either more or less than what the Bible teaches.

Matthew 24:32–44

Next, let's look at part of Jesus's long message to his disciples about his second coming, as told by the Gospel writer Matthew. The courtroom tool helps us avoid saying too much or not enough about this much-debated event.

READ!

Read Matthew 24:32–44. What truths about Jesus's second coming does he make absolutely clear? Think about what is less clear from this passage—and the way that Jesus calls his followers to respond to his teaching.

How might people want to say more than what the Bible says about Jesus's return? They might read Matthew 24:32–33 and note that we will be able to see signs of the coming of Jesus Christ to earth. But they might ignore verse 36, which states very clearly that "no one" except God the Father knows the exact day and hour when Jesus will return to judge the world. Those who ignore this verse and rely only on verses 32–33 may begin to try to guess the exact time or place that Jesus will return, and even make specific plans (and teach in specific ways) about their beliefs in this area. This is clearly saying more than what the Bible says. Sadly, many people have deceived entire groups of believers with specific teachings about the timing of Jesus's return; they have claimed to know more than what the Bible tells us about the end of the world, so they have been guilty of adding to the revelation of Scripture.

However, other people might focus on verse 36 and say, "Well, we will never be able to tell when Jesus will return." Therefore, they may not notice the signs that will precede his coming and will not work hard to stay ready and awake for it. Some might even ignore the coming reality of Jesus's return and neglect the Bible's teaching and reminders that this day is coming soon. This is clearly saying much less than what the Bible teaches. This passage not only says that there are signs that we can look for, but it also reminds Christians to be "awake" and "ready" (vv. 42, 44) for Jesus to return. Christians are supposed to remember Christ's coming, look for it, and prepare for it.

So how do we use the courtroom tool well as we study passages like this in the Gospels? We recognize that we will not be able to know or predict the exact timing of Jesus's return (that is making sure to not say more than what the Bible says), but we look for signs that remind us he is coming back, and we work hard to be ready for his return (that is making sure to not say less than what the Bible says).

Matthew 26:6–13

As we close this chapter, we are going to focus on another passage from Matthew, but we are going to think together about how the courtroom tool can be applied to a concept rather than just one specific passage. We are going to consider the Christian response to people who are poor. This is a big concept, and we will certainly not answer every question about it. But we will try to see some ways that people can say more or less than what the Bible says about this important subject. Our goal, then, is to let the passage from Matthew shape our approach to helping the poor.

READ!

Read Matthew 26:6–13. Think about the implications of Jesus's comments about the poor. Consider how some people might be tempted to say more or less than the teaching of God's word in this passage.

First, let's think through two very extreme perspectives about how to treat people who are poor in a physical or material way. Then we will seek to let Matthew 26 guide us to an approach to this subject that uses the courtroom tool well.

Some people say less than what God's word says about generously helping and giving to people who are poor. People holding this perspective might teach that because the focus of the Bible (and of Jesus's ministry) is about teaching and inviting people to repent of sin and believe in him, helping people tangibly with money and food is not essential for Christians. The only important thing, in their view, is telling people about Jesus (caring for their souls rather than helping their physical condition). This is an example of saying less than what God's word teaches about the poor, because as we look at the entire witness of the Bible, we find many places where God's people are called to help those who are sick, suffering, and even physically poor.

Other people say more than what God's word says about helping people who are poor. People holding this perspective might teach that the biblical call to bring help and justice to those who are in poverty is so apparent, it must become the greatest focus for followers of Jesus Christ. They might say that what it means to be a Christian is to fight for justice for poor people and to help them in any way they can—even if we do not tell them about salvation through Jesus Christ. This is obviously saying more than what God's word teaches about the poor—the Bible clearly does not lift helping the poor to a higher level than telling people about the salvation that comes through Jesus Christ alone.

So how can we use the courtroom tool well to interpret and apply Matthew 26:6–13 on this important subject of helping the poor? This passage shows us that Jesus is certainly not opposed to helping the poor; in fact, he tells his disciples that there will "always" be poor people with them (v. 11), implying that it is very good and important for his disciples to help such people. But as Jesus considers the sacrifice and offering that the woman has given to him by pouring out the perfume, he tells his disciples that she has done the right thing. This woman has focused on worshiping and bowing down before Jesus as her Savior and King. In this moment, that is the most important thing. Jesus is central, and the first call of God's people is to help other people come to him in worship and obedience. But in their worship and obedience to Jesus, it is certainly good for them to care generously for the poor people in their midst, combining gospel proclamation with physical and tangible help and generosity.

REVIEW

In this chapter, you have learned about another important tool that will help you read, study, interpret, and apply the Bible faithfully: the courtroom tool. The purpose of this tool is to help you stay focused on speaking the truth, the whole truth, and nothing but the truth about God's word—just like a good witness in a courtroom. Far too often, people end up saying or teaching more or less than what the Bible says. Faithful students of the Bible seek to stay on the line of faithful teaching. In other words, we must have a balanced interpretation of the Bible, holding certain truths with the right tension.

PRAY!

End this chapter with prayer, committing your study of the Bible to God and asking him to always guide you as you seek to understand and apply his word. Ask him to give you strength to work hard to say neither more nor less than what his word teaches so that you will remain faithful to what he wants you to know, believe, and do.

Chapter 4

THE CRUX TOOL

In chapter 1, I introduced you to six habits for successful Bible study, including "Identify 'core' terms." This habit can help you get closer to the "crux"—the main point, big idea, or central theme—of a Bible passage. Just as every passage has a main point, so does every biblical book, and it's very important to find it. The crux tool—our next hermeneutical tool, which is our focus in this chapter—can help you do that. By using it well, you can discover the message or theme of any biblical book.

Remember!

Your suggested memory verses for this chapter come from the end of one of the books we will look at in this chapter—Jude:

Now to him who is able to keep you from stumbling and to present you blameless before the presence of his glory with great joy, to the only God, our Savior, through Jesus Christ our Lord, be glory, majesty, dominion, and authority, before all time and now and forever. Amen. (Jude 24–25)

UNDERSTANDING THIS TOOL

The idea of finding the main theme or big idea for an entire book of the Bible may seem intimidating because some of those books are very long. So in this section, I want to give you a few basic hints about how you can begin working to identify the crux of *any* book of the Bible by using this tool. This is a very important tool, and here is why: every author of the Bible was inspired by God's Holy Spirit to write, and they wrote with a very clear purpose—a big idea. Unless we identify that big idea—that crux—for any particular book, we will become confused as we study the individual passages within that book. We need to have a good grasp of the overarching point in order to understand the points of the individual parts. The crux tool will help you do that—and will serve you well as you study smaller passages within any book.

Here are the hints that you can use to help you as you seek to pinpoint the crux of a book:

Purpose statement. You can look for a purpose statement. Some biblical authors make it very easy on us; they obviously and openly tell us why they are writing the book and what their main point will be. We will see some examples of this when we begin looking at books of the Bible later in this chapter.

Beginning and ending. You can look at how a book begins and ends. Many times, a biblical author will start by giving you an idea of the main purpose or crux of his book, then will conclude with a restatement of that point. Again, this is a very helpful way to find the crux. It's not very different from the way that many of us were taught to write essays in school—by giving an introduction that states the main point, writing the body of the essay, and then restating the main point in the conclusion. Some biblical authors do this more explicitly than others.

Repetition. You can often discover words, phrases, and ideas that keep coming up throughout a book of the Bible. Many times, what the author keeps repeating is an important hint as to the overall crux of the book.

Obviously, a key part of using these three hints is actually taking some time to read through books of the Bible—even multiple times—and ideally in one sitting. The best method by which to find your way to the crux of a book is to read it again and again, and to work hard to determine the book's shape, trajectory, and major themes. You will get better at using this tool the more you read the Bible. Don't cheat yourself out of the experience of actually reading an entire book of the Bible all the way through; there is no shortcut to good Bible study.

Remember, this tool is a very important one for your tool belt because you cannot understand the various parts of a book unless you grasp the crux of the entire book.

PROBLEMS AVOIDED WITH THIS TOOL

As we have done in previous chapters, let's now think about some problems in Bible interpretation and application that can be avoided when we use the crux tool well. Seeing these problems will set us up to learn about the important benefits of this tool.

What are some of the problems that can happen if we ignore the crux tool as we study biblical books?

We might get lost in our reading and understanding. Perhaps you have known the experience of getting lost in your reading or study of a particular book. If this has ever happened to you, you know that it is not fun; rather, it's quite frustrating. It is not pleasant to be confused or to not understand what an author is doing or where he or she is going with a plot or a story. Understanding the crux of a biblical book will help you avoid getting lost as you read and study it. It will help you keep the main focus central in your mind so you can always look for the way the author is developing, expanding, or referring to that main point.

We might fail to see the right application in our study. Sometimes as we study a particular passage in the Bible, we begin to think that it is leading to a particular application for Christian actions, thoughts, or words. But we are not sure. How do we know if we are applying a Bible passage to our lives in the right way? One way we can check our application is to see if it lines up with the overall crux of the book. If it fits with the main point that the author is making, there is a good chance that it is a good application. But if it is completely off the crux of the book, we likely have understood some verses incorrectly.

We might miss the main point of the entire book. Finally, if we do not *first* work on finding the main point of a book by putting the crux tool to work, we may discover that we have worked through a book passage by passage and missed the book's big idea. That would not be a good thing. Putting the crux tool to work first can help us get a big picture of the main point of the book. Then, as we work through it passage by passage, we can see the way each individual passage relates to the overall big idea that the author is trying to communicate.

BENEFITS RECEIVED WITH THIS TOOL

Now let's think about some benefits that can come from using the crux tool well.

Hearing the main "melody" of the book. In musical pieces, there is almost always a main melody that is repeated throughout. There are pieces of harmony that are combined with this melody, but the melody serves as the main musical theme for the entire piece. Books of the Bible can be much like this. There are often many elements of harmony that combine with the main theme, and there are different variations of the big idea that the author is trying to get across. But ultimately there is one main melody that the book really centers on—its main message. The crux tool is ideal for helping Bible students find their way to that main melody so that they will keep their focus on the main point of the biblical author.

Understanding the author's intention. The above point leads us to a second important benefit of the crux tool. When this tool is used well in a book of the Bible, the Bible student can actually see the main intention of the biblical author. He or she can begin to discern what the author is trying to do in different parts of the biblical book. This is the best way to "get inside the heads" of the writers of Scripture, to see their books from their perspective. Also, as we learned previously in connection with the context tool, finding the intention of the original author—and the perspective of the original audience—is key to making sure that we get our interpretation and application of Scripture right.

Connecting individual passages. Perhaps the greatest benefit of using the crux tool well is that, when the big idea of a book is located, it helps you connect the biblical passages in the book to one another because you can see how they are all relating to—or expanding on—the overall theme of the book. Passages in a biblical book change from being random stories, arguments, or poems to being important pieces in the overall point that the book is making for its audience. In other words, the crux tool can help bring a good, grounded perspective on every part of the book, which will help you in your study of each individual section.

APPLYING THIS TOOL

Using the hints that I mentioned at the beginning of the chapter, let's now put the crux tool to work in the study of several Bible books. As in the application sections in previous chapters, you will begin by reading a passage or verse (or several of each), then seek to interpret it faithfully by putting the tool to work. The goal is to give you practice in finding the crux of any book of the Bible in order to grow in your ability to study, interpret, and apply it well.

The Book of Jude

We'll look first at the little book of Jude.

READ!

Read the entire book of Jude; it is only twenty-five verses long. Read this letter carefully and make observations as you go—they might help you find your way to the crux of this book.

Let's think about our three hints for finding the crux of a biblical book in relation to Jude.

First, did you find a purpose statement? There is one in Jude 3! Jude begins his letter by telling his audience that he wanted to write to them about the "common salvation" that they share, but he felt that he needed to write to them instead about the need to "contend" for their faith in Jesus Christ. So the purpose statement of this book leads us to believe that "contending" for the Christian faith will be at least a major part of the crux that Jude focuses on as he writes.

Second, did you notice any similarities between the way this book begins and the way it ends? In both the beginning and the end, Jude focuses on the word "keep" or "kept." He begins by addressing people who are "kept" for Jesus Christ (v. 1) and ends by reminding these people that God can "keep" them blameless until the end (v. 24). Ultimately, according to Jude, God will keep his true people safe until the end; he will accomplish his salvation in their lives.

Third, did you find repetition of any words, phrases, or themes? Much of the book contains examples and warnings about people who have turned away from God and rejected faith in Jesus Christ in favor of sin. Jude mentions the unbelievers in the midst of the people of Israel (v. 5), the cities of Sodom and Gomorrah (v. 7), and the evil prophet Balaam (v. 11). This repetition of bad examples seems to lead us closer to the reason that Jude is calling his audience to contend for their faith.

So how does all of this come together to lead us to the crux of the book of Jude? We might say that Jude seems to be about this important truth and call: God's people must *contend* for their faith even as they are *kept* until the end by a powerful God. There is an element of warning to this call, which is why Jude cites so many negative examples of people who have failed to contend for the faith and have fallen into sin and rebellion. God's true people, according to Jude, must fight to hold on to the true gospel, but they must do so trusting that their good God will ultimately keep their faith true and strong until the end. It seems we have landed with firm footing on the basic crux of Jude's letter.

The Gospel of John

Jude is a very short biblical book, so let's now put the crux tool to work in a much longer one: the Gospel of John. Don't worry—I'm not going to ask you to read this entire Gospel at once (at least not right now)! Instead, you'll read just a couple of key passages that will help you get a good sense of what the crux of this book might be. Obviously, if you were doing a full study on the Gospel of John, it would be good to read the entire book.

READ!

Read John 20:30–31. Read those verses several times, thinking about what this clear purpose statement might be telling you about the crux of this Gospel. Then skim over the story of Jesus's meeting and conversation with the woman at the well in John 4. Think about how this story relates to the purpose statement in 20:30–31.

Now that you've read the passages above, let's begin forming a good guess about what the crux of this book might be. Of course, you can study the Gospel of John in much more detail to see if we have gotten this crux correct based on our brief reading and study.

First, consider John's purpose statement in chapter 20. John makes it very easy on us as readers, doesn't he? He tells us specifically *why* he has written his Gospel. He says he has done this so that his readers might come to "believe" that Jesus is the Son of God, and that through that belief, they might have "life" in his name (v. 31). From this clear purpose statement, we can begin to put the first pieces of the crux of the Gospel of John in place since we know why John is writing. The crux, it seems, must have something to do with both belief and life.

Second, think about John 4, which you skimmed over. Jesus has an amazing conversation with a Samaritan woman at a well, and two big themes emerge from it: belief and life. Jesus begins to talk to this woman about "living" water, which will help her never be thirsty again (vv. 10–14). He goes on to make this amazing statement: "The water that I will give him will become in him a spring of water welling up to eternal life" (v. 14). Jesus makes a huge claim here; he embraces the authority to give eternal life to people. Then look at what happens next. First, the woman believes in Jesus as the Savior, the Messiah of the world (v. 42). Then many people from her town believe in him as well as they listen to this woman talk about Jesus (v. 39). Do you see? John's two big themes—belief and life—show up in this story in John 4.

So to summarize, we might say—through looking at just John's purpose statement and this one passage—that the crux of the Gospel of John is this: *Belief* in Jesus Christ as the *Son of God* leads to eternal *life*. That is what John intends to focus on in his Gospel. So in every passage we study in the Gospel of John, we should be sure to ask, "How is this passage relating to the importance of belief in Jesus Christ and the life that comes only through acceptance of him as the Son of God?" Once we get the crux, our study of each passage in the book becomes easier and clearer—and it becomes more difficult to stray from the main point and main application of the biblical author.

The Gospel of Luke

We've now seen how a clear purpose statement from a biblical author can be very important and helpful in identifying a crux for a biblical book. John explicitly tells his readers that he writes everything in his Gospel so that they will come to belief in Jesus Christ as the Son of God, and so that, through that belief, they will have eternal life. That purpose statement helps us read every part of his Gospel with great focus and understanding.

Luke has a different focus in his Gospel, but his purpose statement is similarly helpful; he also clearly identifies his reason for writing. Yet in the Gospel of Luke, we have to dig a little deeper than in John in order to find the full crux of the book. To do that, we'll look at a few key passages from this Gospel.

READ!

Read the following three passages from the book of Luke. They will put you on a good path toward finding the crux of this Gospel. Read:

- *Luke 1:1–4—Luke's initial purpose statement for the book*
- *Luke 15—a great description of the ministry of Jesus that Luke seeks to highlight in his Gospel*
- *Luke 24:44–49—Luke's record of some of Jesus's final words to his disciples before his ascension into heaven*

As you read these passages from the Gospel of Luke, try to put together the themes and ideas that Luke seems to be focused on in every one of them. How do these contribute to our understanding of the crux of this book?

First, consider Luke 1:1–4, the introduction to Luke's Gospel, where we find his purpose statement. This passage is addressed to a man named Theophilus (possibly a wealthy saint who had provided from his means to enable Luke to write this Gospel account). What is Luke's focus here? The focus is on "certainty" (v. 4). Luke says that his goal was to put together an "orderly" account (v. 3) of everything that happened in the life and work of Jesus Christ so that Theophilus will have certainty about everything that he has heard and been taught. Luke is writing so that people will be sure about Jesus—so that they will know the truth of his coming, his death, and his resurrection. So certainty must be part of the crux of this book. But that is not all.

Second, consider Luke 15, a famous chapter about three lost things—a sheep, a coin, and a son. The chapter begins with the Pharisees grumbling about Jesus because he is going to "sinners," whom they see as unclean and without hope (v. 2). Jesus tells these three parables to make it clear to these grumbling Pharisees that he has come for everyone—for all nations, all peoples, and especially sinners who are in need of his saving grace. Jesus even inserts a character into the final parable—the older brother of the prodigal son—who grumbles at his father's grace toward his sinful brother (v. 30). It is as if Jesus is pointing a finger at the Pharisees and saying, "I have come to save sinners, and it is not right that you should grumble about this; all heaven rejoices when sinners turn to me and are saved!" So it seems that the salvation of lost people—from everywhere—is a major part of Jesus's ministry that Luke highlights in his Gospel.

Third, think about the last passage of the three you read. As Jesus begins to say goodbye to his disciples, he explains to them that everything that has happened—his death for sins and his resurrection from the dead—came about in order to fulfill the Scriptures and God's great promises to his people (Luke 24:44–46). In other words, all has been "accomplished," as Luke said in 1:1 (notice the same theme appearing at both the beginning and end of the book, one of our three hints for finding the crux). The point of this accomplishment, though, according to Jesus, is that "repentance for the forgiveness of sins should be proclaimed in his name to all nations" (v. 47). So what is the purpose of the certainty about what Jesus has accomplished? According to Jesus (and Luke), the purpose is that salvation in his name should be proclaimed to all nations, all people, and all sinners who need God's grace. That is how Luke ends his Gospel.

So when we put these three key passages from the Gospel of Luke together, where do we land for a crux for this Gospel? It might be something like this: We should be certain that Jesus really has accomplished salvation for sinners through his death on the cross, and that certainty should lead us to proclaim the gospel to all people everywhere! To put it more simply, we might say that the crux of the Gospel of Luke is "Gospel certainty, which leads to gospel proclamation to all people and all nations."

The Gospel of Matthew

Let's now look together at some key passages from one more Gospel—Matthew. This book, like John and Luke, contains some very clear hints about the crux that its author intends to focus on.

READ!

As in your study of the Gospel of Luke, I'd like you to read three passages from the Gospel of Matthew in order to begin forming an idea of the book's crux. See if you can begin to find a common theme through these readings:

- *Matthew 1:1–17—Matthew's introduction of Jesus to his audience*
- *Matthew 7:28–29—Matthew's conclusion of the account of Jesus's teaching in his Sermon on the Mount*
- *Matthew 28:16–20—the words of Jesus, recorded by Matthew, as he sends out his disciples to make more disciples*

What do we see when we look at these passages?

First, we see that Matthew begins his Gospel with a genealogy (1:1–17). You may not know much about the significance of this kind of a beginning, but the people of Matthew's day would have immediately seen what he was doing. Only important people were introduced with a genealogy, so Matthew is saying that he is about to tell the story of a very important person. There is even more than this: Matthew traces Jesus's genealogy back to Abraham through David. By starting this way, Matthew is presenting Jesus as a person in a kingly line. He is a man with power and *authority*.

Second, think about the way that Matthew wraps up Jesus's famous time of teaching that is often referred to as the Sermon on the Mount (chaps. 5–7). What amazes the crowds about this teaching of Jesus? It is not just the content of his teaching, but also the "authority" with which he teaches it (7:29). Jesus does not teach like their scribes and religious leaders but as if he really owns the right to interpret—with authority—God's word to God's people. Matthew is again setting up Jesus as the one who has *authority*—this time relating to teaching the Bible.

Third, remember the way that Jesus sends off his disciples to bear witness to him in all the world and make disciples of him (28:18–20). He begins by saying that "all authority in heaven and on earth" has been given to him (v. 18). Matthew is now being extremely clear. He has told the story of the Son of God who came into the world with kingly authority, taught God's word with authority, died, and rose again, and who now sends his disciples off into the world with all authority. Are you getting the point?

So while we do not have a clear purpose statement in the Gospel of Matthew, we can begin finding our way to the crux—*the authority of Jesus as the Son of God*—by looking at both the beginning and end of the book and the repetition of the theme of kingly rule and authority.

The Book of Romans

By now you should be able to see how the crux tool can help you get a grasp of the overall point of a book in the Bible so that you are better equipped to study every part of it.

Next, let's put this tool to work in the book that many consider to be the theologically richest in the entire Bible (and the one with the clearest and most systematic explanation of the gospel): Paul's letter to the Romans. There is no way that we could ever study Romans in the kind of depth it requires in just a few pages. But we are going to see how looking at some of the hints we have learned about can help us make our way quickly toward the crux of this book.

READ!

Once again, I'd like you to read three selections from the book of Romans in order to get a picture of what the crux of this marvelous and difficult book might be:

- *Romans 1:1–7—the way that Paul introduces this book and frames his discussion, which he begins in the following chapters*
- *Romans 3:21–26—the center of Paul's gospel proclamation and explanation, summarizing the gospel of Jesus Christ in a beautiful and powerful way*
- *Romans 16:25–27—the doxology that Paul uses to conclude this great book*

As you read these passages, think about how they are brought together by common themes and about how you might learn from them about the crux of the book of Romans.

Now that you have read the above passages, we will make a first move toward a crux for this book.

First, consider the opening of Paul's letter to the Romans—1:1–7. Paul introduces himself and says very clearly that he has been "set apart for the gospel of God" (v. 1). Paul's letter will be about the gospel—we could have guessed that! But also pay attention to the rest of the language Paul uses in this introduction. His goal, he says, is to "bring about the *obedience of faith*" as he proclaims the gospel (v. 5). Then he adds another important phrase: he wants this faith to happen "among *all the nations*." Keep these things in mind as we turn to the next passage. Paul is about the gospel, of course, but also the "obedience of faith" in "all nations."

Second, consider the heart of the message of the gospel in Romans 3:21–26. Paul intentionally places all people—Jews and Gentiles—together under sin; "all have sinned," he writes (v. 23). But he also makes very clear that the only way to receive God's salvation is through "faith in Jesus Christ for all who believe" (v. 22). So faith is the key. This is the very heart of the gospel; it is about what Jesus Christ did on the cross for all people who repent of sin and put their faith in him as the Savior.

Third, think about the very end of the book—the final blessing from Paul in 16:25–27. He closes by talking about the "preaching of

Jesus Christ"—the gospel (v. 25). But two familiar elements come up again (we are using our "beginning and ending" tool). First, he says that the message of Jesus Christ has been made known to "all nations" (v. 26). Second, he says that God's goal in the gospel is to bring about the "obedience of faith" (v. 26). Remember those two phrases?

So as we read and study just these three short passages from the book of Romans, putting to work the hints that we have learned, we can come to at least a first good guess about the crux of this book. Romans, it seems, is about the *gospel* of Jesus Christ, which is for people from *all nations* who will *obey* God through *faith* in his Son. That seems to be Paul's focus as he writes this rich letter to the church in Rome.

The Book of Leviticus

Before we close this chapter, we are going to look at a book that you might not have expected to study as part of the application of the crux tool: Leviticus. However, you are going to find that this book is quite a good one for practice with this tool. Many people avoid it because of the long lists of laws, but it is surprisingly clear in its big idea and in its relevance for Christians who study it. Let's dive in.

READ!

I'd like you to read several passages and verses from Leviticus because we are going to focus mainly on the hint of repetition. As you look at the following verses, see if you begin to notice any common words, phrases, themes, or ideas that point to the crux of this book:

- *Leviticus 4:22–26*
- *Leviticus 15:31*
- *Leviticus 16:1–5*
- *Leviticus 19:1*
- *Leviticus 19:37*

Let's think about the repetition we find in these passages and verses.

First, we see the theme of "uncleanness" coming up again and again. It seems from these passages and verses (and from other parts of the book of Leviticus) that there is an almost infinite number of ways that God's people can become unclean and separated from him. Diseases, certain behaviors and foods, and, of course, sin can all put God's people in that dangerous place.

Second, we see that God provides many methods for his people to become ceremonially "clean" and acceptable for him. There are washing rituals and, of course, there are sacrifices that even the priests need to make to cover their sin. God provides the way for his people to be washed, made clean, and forgiven—and that kind of cleanliness and purity seems to be tied to their acceptability to God as they approach him in worship.

Third, especially in Leviticus 19:2, we see the overall theme that seems to summarize much of what God is commanding his people in the book of Leviticus. They are to be "holy," or set apart, just as God is "holy." God is calling his people to be set apart for him; he is holy, so they must live set-apart lives if they want to dwell in close proximity with this kind of God.

Fourth, we see that every command that God gives to his people is grounded in who he is; God says that he commands his people to do certain things because "I am the Lord" (see Lev. 19:37 for example). So the actions of his people are commanded because of the perfect character of the holy God who reigns over his people. His character—his holiness—is the chief motivation for their obedience and worship.

So what might the crux of Leviticus be? We might state it like this: Leviticus is about God's people being called to be holy, cleansed, and set apart for life with an infinitely holy God. Christians today have much to learn about God's holiness from this book, as well as about the ultimate cleansing that happens through the blood of Jesus Christ—the perfect sacrifice for God's sinful people (which the book of Leviticus so clearly anticipates and foreshadows).

REVIEW

You have learned in this chapter about a very important tool for Bible interpretation and application—the crux tool. This tool is designed to help you find your way to the main point or big idea of an entire book in the Bible. By using certain hints (the book's purpose statement, themes that recur at the beginning and ending, and repetition of words, phrases, and ideas), we can quickly discover the crux of what biblical authors are trying to communicate to us as they write their books.

PRAY!

As you end this chapter in prayer, spend a few minutes talking to God about your approach to studying his word. Ask him to help you study it not just for knowledge, but also because you want to know him better and love him more. As you grow in your understanding of the crux of books in the Bible, ask God to help you also grow in your love for him—the God who inspired every word of the Scriptures that you read and study.

Chapter 5

THE CONSTRUCTION TOOL

Every passage in the Bible has a structure. The human authors of Scripture were inspired to write by God's Holy Spirit, but they wrote with careful attention to organization and structure; in other words, they did not write haphazardly, randomly, or chaotically. Often, however, we do not work hard to actually find the structure of the biblical passages that we study. We simply read them and ask general questions—or make general comments—about them, or we focus on the impressions or feelings that biblical passages give us. When we study this way, failing to pay attention to the structure of the passages we are focusing on, we run the risk of making incorrect interpretations and applications.

To counteract that danger, we need to add the *construction* tool to our hermeneutical tool belts. This tool, the fourth of the six we are considering in this book, is our focus for this chapter.

Think about the tools that we have studied so far:

- The *context* tool. We considered the fact that every text in the Bible has a specific context, which we need to think about carefully in order to come to the right interpretation and application.
- The *courtroom* tool. We saw that we need to always seek the truth, the whole truth, and nothing but the truth about any given Bible passage—not less and not more.
- The *crux* tool. We considered an approach to study that seeks to find the crux (the main point or big idea) of an entire biblical book in order to understand every part of that book better.

These important tools are designed to help you read, understand, and apply the Bible well. They are not tools for Bible *study* specifically; rather, they are principles that should shape your interpretation and application of the biblical text.

As we learn about the construction tool, I want to begin by introducing you to the key concept behind this tool and to the principles of biblical interpretation that undergird it.

Remember!

The suggested memory verses for this chapter come from Psalm 19—a "love song" about God's word. It's a wonderful psalm to point us toward the attitude we ought to have toward the Scriptures, which are given to us (and carefully organized for us) by our good and gracious God.

The law of the Lord is perfect, reviving the soul; the testimony of the Lord is sure, making wise the simple; the precepts of the Lord are right, rejoicing the heart; the commandment of the Lord is pure, enlightening the eyes; the fear of the Lord is clean, enduring forever; the rules of the Lord are true, and righteous altogether. (Ps. 19:7–9)

UNDERSTANDING THIS TOOL

The construction tool is designed to help you find the *structure* (or the shape) of any given passage in the Bible in order to find your way to its true meaning, purpose, and application.

This tool operates on the basis that every passage in the Bible has a structure, and the structure is important because it shows us the *focus* or *thrust* of the passage. In other words, the way the biblical author puts a passage together can show us what that author means to emphasize, highlight, and bring out for his readers. Very often, the structure of a passage is the main key to interpreting it well, understanding it rightly, and applying it faithfully to our lives. This is why the construction tool is so important—it helps us see what the biblical authors want us to see.

What are some ways that we can begin to see the structure, or construction, of a passage in the Bible? We can do the following:

- Look for key words (such as *so*, *therefore*, *if*, or *since*) and phrases (such as "In conclusion" or "Because of this . . ."). Those kinds of key transition words and phrases often help us see the way a passage is put together.
- Look for changes in subject or topic; when an author shifts from one topic to another, that is usually an indication of the way he is structuring his thoughts or argument.
- Look for repeated words. Repetition of words in key places in a biblical text can offer a hint as to the structure of that text.

In the next few pages, we will look at some problems that the construction tool helps us avoid in our study of the Bible, as well as some benefits it provides when we put it to work in good ways. After that, we will begin using this valuable tool as we study passages from the Bible and see how it helps us in our study and grasp of the biblical authors' emphases and main points.

PROBLEMS AVOIDED WITH THIS TOOL

The construction tool is not simply a fun and helpful addition to your hermeneutical tool belt (although it is); it also can protect you from some serious errors and misunderstandings about the Bible. As I noted briefly above, we often read and study Scripture simply to hear it and see how it makes us feel rather than to discern the way a biblical author has intentionally put words together in order to teach us. Now, hearing the Bible and being emotionally moved by it are, of course, good things. There are certainly times when we should simply sit and listen to the Bible, or read it devotionally, without the kind of careful study that we are learning about in this book. But as I hope to convince you, there are also times to study the Bible carefully in order to understand what it really means (given its context, structure, etc.), and therefore, how we should apply it as Christians today. That's where the construction tool comes in. It is extremely important for helping you rightly understand the main point and main application of any passage in Scripture.

What are some problems in Bible interpretation and application that can be avoided when we use the construction tool well?

Misplaced emphasis. First, by rightly applying this tool, you can avoid the problem of misplaced emphasis. As we noted earlier, the structure—or construction—of a passage is almost always a very important key to understanding its focus, main point, or emphasis. The biblical authors put their writing together in intentional ways in order to help us see what they were emphasizing. If we do not work hard to put the construction tool to work—to find the structure of the biblical passages that we study—we are in danger of finding emphasis in any given passage in a place where the author never intended it. We might stumble on a biblical truth and yet completely miss the *central* truth that a Bible passage is intended to teach us.

Wandering thoughts. Second, you can avoid the problem of wandering thoughts. Some students of the Bible tend to just read along without really thinking carefully about the meaning of the passage before them, much less its organization. Sometimes when we read the Bible this way, we almost get the impression that the biblical authors simply wrote random thoughts, putting down whatever words happened to pop into their minds. That could not be further from the truth. The biblical authors worked hard to carefully craft their writing; they were not just recording their wandering thoughts or jotting down words in a stream-of-consciousness kind of way. As we study the structure of their writing carefully, we will be guarded against thinking that the Bible was put together randomly.

Literary abuse. Third, you can avoid the problem of literary abuse when you apply this tool faithfully. This final point is very important. If we do not work hard to find the structure of biblical books, we are actually doing literary damage to the Bible, which is a literary book. Because real human authors wrote the Bible, even as they were inspired by God's Holy Spirit, we should expect that they wrote in logical and organized ways. To fail to look for the construction of their writings is to fail to respect the Bible as a true *literary* work—even one that is also God's *inspired* word.

BENEFITS RECEIVED WITH THIS TOOL

Now let's shift our focus to the great benefits that come to your Bible interpretation and application when you use the construction tool well in your study. I want you to see some of the important insights that this tool can give you and to come to understand why I am placing such emphasis on construction in this chapter.

Here are some of the benefits of using the construction tool:

Finding the author's outline. Have you ever written a paper for school? If so, you probably had some kind of outline as you prepared to write. You knew, for example, that you would begin with an introductory paragraph, then move on to talk about several points (logically in order), and then end with a paragraph of conclusion. The biblical authors also had outlines as they wrote, and the construction tool can help you find them. When we put this tool to work carefully, we can begin to discover the way the biblical authors were putting their writing together in order to allow it to flow out logically and with good organization. When we uncover their outlines, it is then much easier for us to understand what they are saying and how we should apply it.

Finding the author's emphasis. Far too often, as we read and study the Bible, we place a lot of emphasis on things that just happen to jump out at us as we read. Perhaps a certain word strikes us from a passage; all of a sudden, we become very focused on that word and begin to think about it as the most important part of the passage. That can often be very dangerous. It is the structure of a passage that actually shows us what the author is emphasizing—not just what happens to jump out at us as we read. Careful work with the construction tool to discover the structure of a passage is key to seeing what the author is building toward—the key point that he wants us, the readers, to focus on.

Discovering the right application. The construction tool also can help you apply a Bible passage in the way that the human (and divine) author intends. This is the most practical benefit of this tool. By discovering the structure of a Bible passage, we find the main focus (or emphasis) of the biblical author; that emphasis then leads us to the right application of the passage to our lives. Have you thought deeply about this? Seeing the construction of a passage is the way that you discover how you are to apply God's word to your life. This makes the construction tool extremely important.

APPLYING THIS TOOL

Let's now put the construction tool to work in the study of several Bible passages. In each of these application examples, you will begin by reading the verse or passage, then seek to interpret the verse or passage faithfully by putting the tool to work. The goal is to give you good practice in finding the structure of passages you might study in every part of the Bible.

Psalm 19

We'll begin by using the construction tool to find the structure of the beautiful Psalm 19. The goal, of course, is more than simply finding the way that this psalm is constructed, although that will be an important part of what you will do. The bigger goal is to find the right interpretation and application of this psalm to your life; these will both come through a good understanding of its carefully crafted structure.

READ!

Read Psalm 19 carefully, slowly, and thoughtfully. Pay attention to the topics and themes that are discussed. Look for changes in focus, which might signal different sections of the psalm; these changes will help you understand the writer's construction plan as he put this psalm together. Begin thinking about how the organization of this psalm might point you to a good interpretation and application of it.

How is Psalm 19 put together?

First, we find that verses 1–6 seem to go together as the first section of this psalm. These verses are about the way that the world—God's creation—"speaks" about his glory, majesty, and power.

Second, we find that verses 7–11 seem to go together as the second section of this psalm. These verses are about the way that the word—God's law—speaks about his holiness, goodness, and perfection. So while the *world* points to God's glory, the *word* points more specifically to his holiness.

Third, we find that verses 12–14 seem to go together as the third and final section of this psalm. These verses seem to be the psalmist's conclusion to both the way the world speaks about God and the way the word speaks about him. As the psalmist reacts to the messages of God's world (his glory) and God's word (his holiness), his response is to cry out for God to declare him "innocent" (v. 12). In other words, God's glory and holiness remind the psalmist of his sin and his need to be declared innocent by the perfect and holy God. The psalm ends with a prayer that God would help the psalmist be "acceptable" (or "pleasing," v. 14) to him in every way—with the words of his mouth and the meditation of his heart. You might say that verses 12–14 are the main application—the psalmist's prayer to God—based on the theological truths that are declared in the first two sections of the psalm.

Do you see how we found our way to the construction of this psalm? We uncovered the psalmist's outline. If we miss the careful structure, we might be able to pick out some truths about God and about us from this psalm, but we would miss the shape, the progression of thought, and potentially the main point! He writes to show how both the "book" of God's world and the "book" of God's word are designed to teach us about who God is (his glory and his holiness). Then he shows us the only right response to the glorious and holy God: it is a plea and prayer for God to save us and declare us innocent, followed by an expression of commitment to follow him in every area of life. This response is the proper application of this psalm for us today as we seek to follow Jesus Christ, who alone *can* declare us innocent and righteous before our glorious and holy God through his saving work in our place.

Luke 15

Let's now turn to a passage from the Gospel of Luke that also has a very clear construction. Luke definitely put it together with much care and precision. Even more than with Psalm 19, the message of this passage shines through as we see its structure. You could even say that it is difficult to understand what this passage is about *without* seeing Luke's construction of it.

READ!

Read Luke 15—the entire chapter. As you read, do your best to notice the construction of this passage. How is it put together? What are the different parts? How do they relate to one another? As you begin to see the shape of this passage, start thinking about how that shape affects the chapter's meaning and emphasis. What does Luke want his readers to focus on in this passage?

Luke begins by giving the setting in which Jesus tells parables in this chapter. Jesus is ministering to "tax collectors and sinners," who are "drawing near to hear him" (v. 1). The Pharisees, though, are not happy about this. In fact, they grumble at the fact that Jesus is receiving these sinful people. This grumbling causes Jesus to respond by telling three parables. Let's look at the structure of these parables. What are their main parts?

- In each parable, something is *lost*. A sheep is lost; a coin is lost; a son is lost. This is the problem in each parable.
- In each parable, something is *found*. The sheep is found; the coin is found; the son is found. This is the good news Jesus uses in each parable to represent his ministry and work on earth.
- In each parable, there is *rejoicing* after the lost thing is found. In the first two accounts, the people call their friends together to celebrate with them, and in the third parable, the father throws a huge feast for his lost son who has returned.

So you can see the clear structure that Luke is using in this passage. But there is one more important part of the structure that leads us to Luke's (and Jesus's) emphasis in this section of the Gospel.

Look again at the third parable, which is often called the parable of the prodigal son. It does not simply end with rejoicing, like the first two parables do. What element of structure is added to this parable? It is the grumbling of the older brother (vv. 25–30); that is the great surprise in the structure of this chapter. There should be universal rejoicing that the younger son has returned, but there is not; the older son is upset that his younger brother has been saved and accepted by his loving father.

Where does this added element in the third parable take us? It takes us right back to the beginning of the chapter, where we see the Pharisees grumbling at the ministry of Jesus, who is receiving sinners with love. So what point is Luke making through his construction of the passage? His point is to show that Jesus is focused on saving lost people—and that the salvation of lost sinners ought to bring joy to the hearts of all who truly know, love, and worship him. The Pharisees, though, are not convinced; in fact, they grumble at Jesus's saving work for sinners (those they consider unworthy, dirty, and outside of God's reach). They are not excited about the things that Jesus—and all the angels in heaven—are excited about. These three parables are organized intentionally by Jesus—and Luke as he records them—as a sharp rebuke of the hard hearts of the Pharisees.

This structure would be missed, by the way, if we did not read Luke 15 as one "pericope" (or "literary unit"). Often, half of our work in utilizing this tool is working hard to determine the right length of section to study. In this chapter, for example, the beginning and ending of the chapter clue us into the fact that these three parables are meant to be studied together.

Philippians 2:5–11

I hope you are seeing more and more how noticing the structure of passages from the Bible helps us see their meaning.

Next we'll study a passage from Paul's letter to the Philippians, and you will again see a very clear shape in this passage, one that points us toward the main point that Paul is making. This passage actually has a more picturelike shape; that is, the construction of these verses helps back up and illustrate the theological point that Paul is making about Jesus Christ. Hopefully by the end of this brief study of the passage you will have an even clearer understanding of the descent of Jesus Christ to the earth and to death, and of his glorious resurrection and glorification as the Lord of all.

READ!

Read the passage for this section: Philippians 2:5–11. Read it all the way through at least twice, slowly and carefully. Begin to think about the shape of this passage. How is Paul putting this section together? If you were going to illustrate the structure of these verses with a picture or a diagram, how would you do it? What is this passage teaching about Jesus through this shape and construction?

Let's now apply the construction tool to this passage. Note that Paul begins by calling the Philippian believers to have the same "mind" (v. 5) among themselves that Christ Jesus had—the mind that is theirs through faith in him. The context for this is the situation in the church of Philippi, where there is fighting, strife, and division. People are not doing well at having the mind of Christ, but are putting the people around them down in many ways.

As we look at verses 6–8, then, we see how Paul begins to give a certain direction to these verses as he starts to describe the mind of Christ. What is the direction of these verses? The direction is *downward.* Paul is emphasizing the way that Jesus, the very Son of God, intentionally plunged downward in humility to become human, and even to die on a cross. Each phrase in these verses takes him lower and lower—he makes himself nothing, takes the form of a servant, becomes human, and dies on a cross. The shape of these verses is clearly showing the downward plunge that Jesus Christ takes in order to save sinners through his death on the cross.

But something different happens in verses 9–11. What is the direction of these verses? They show us how Jesus, after his death and resurrection, is raised *upward* in great glory, power, and majesty. God exalts Jesus, and his name is lifted up above every other name in all the earth and in heaven. The passage ends with a declaration that "every tongue" will confess that this Jesus is Lord (v. 11). After showing Jesus's downward plunge into humility, Paul shows us the way that Jesus is then exalted and lifted up to the highest place of glory and honor.

So Paul's construction of this passage is meant to show the Philippians the pattern of Jesus, which they are to follow in their relationships with the people around them. They are to imitate their Savior, who did not grasp power and honor for himself (v. 6), but was willing to humbly go down to the depths—even to death on the cross—in order to serve and save sinners. Christians are called to imitate the shape of their Savior's life and work. There is glory to come—but not before humility, service, and sacrifice. The construction of this passage makes Paul's point to the Philippians loud and clear. The structure of the passage shows us what the biblical author is emphasizing.

Genesis 11:1–9

Next, we will look at Genesis 11:1–9—the account of the construction of the tower of Babel. This is a passage with a very carefully constructed shape; our goal is to find that shape and see what it preaches to us about human sin and the power of God.

READ!

Read Genesis 11:1–9 carefully, slowly, and thoughtfully, making observations about its structure as you go. Think especially about how this passage begins and ends, and about what happens in the very middle. How might the structure be working to make the main point in this passage?

Genesis 11:1–9 is a well-known passage, but many people do not notice its amazing and clear structure—a structure that leads us to its author's clear emphasis.

First, notice the way this passage begins. Verse 1 is a simple statement that during this time "the whole earth had one language and the same words." So the setting for the events in this account is a place where people are multiplying into a mass of humanity that is united by a common language. Sadly, this unity is not a good thing; the people are united not only by language but also by pride and sinful ambition. Eventually they rebel against God.

Second, notice the way that this passage ends. It concludes with the naming of the place as Babel and the summary statement that God "confused" the language of the people and dispersed all of them throughout the face of the earth after their rebellion and sin against him (v. 9). So the beginning and ending show us the general movement of this passage. This is the story of humanity—united in the beginning of the story, with one common language, but separated by the end, dispersed throughout the earth with many different languages.

Third, notice what happens right in the middle of this passage, in verse 5: God comes down. The Lord descends to visit these sinful and rebellious people (which is ironic, because God must come *down* to see the great tower that they are building *upward* toward the heavens). In other words, at the very center of this passage is a reminder that God is in complete control of the situation. He is the King of all the earth, and he is going to reign over even these stubborn and rebellious people. Even the heights of their accomplishment don't reach the glory, majesty, and power of the mighty God who reigns from heaven.

Fourth, notice the way that the words and actions of the people line up with the words and actions of God in this passage. For example, verse 3 and verse 7 seem to be reflections of each other. In verse 3, the people say, "Come," as they talk about building a great tower to the heavens. In verse 7, God says, "Come," as he decides to go down to these sinful people and confuse their language. The language in both of these verses, initiating actions, seems to contain intentional echoes.

I hope you are beginning to see the careful and intentional structure that the author has given to this passage. It is formed as a *chiasm*—a method of organization that causes a narrative to begin and end in the same general place, with each part on either side of the middle reflecting the other (like the words of the people and the words of God in verses

3 and 7). The focal point in a chiasm is the very middle—in this case, God coming down to earth to deal with the people's sin and rebellion. God is not allowing the people to continue in their joint effort of sin. He disperses them into different places of the earth. Ultimately, God does this for their own protection, so that they will not continue to join together in sin in such prideful and arrogant ways.

It's always good to keep your eye out for chiastic shapes in passages of Scripture—there are a lot of them. And remember, the central emphasis in a chiasm tends to be what the author places right in the center of it.

1 Samuel 22

Now let's look at another passage from the Old Testament—1 Samuel 22. This is a passage with a very clear structure. Its construction is designed intentionally to emphasize an important point about God's anointed king, David, in contrast with the reigning king, who is turning against God and his people: Saul. You will see the way that the passage's structure shows us this stark contrast. This contrast can even help us look ahead to the wonderful reign of Christ over his people.

READ!

Read 1 Samuel 22 carefully—the entire chapter. Make sure you are absolutely clear about what is going on. Think about the way the author is intentionally putting this chapter together. What is his construction meant to communicate? How is he structuring this chapter in a way that is designed to teach us about the contrast between these two kings?

First, notice that this passage begins with a picture of David—who has been anointed as king of Israel but is still waiting for God to place him on the throne—gathering outcasts and misfits together with him in a cave. It is not a glamorous life by any means; David is constantly running for his life as the reigning King Saul tries to kill him. But David is pictured here as the one who gives refuge, safety, and a place to belong to people who have been cast out by society and have nowhere else to turn. He is a kind of savior for such people.

Second, in the long, middle section of this passage, Saul—the angry and evil king, who feels his kingdom slipping away from him—turns against a priest who has helped David escape. But Saul goes much further than simply punishing this one priest; he does an unthinkably evil thing. Saul murders eighty-five priests and members of their families because he is so angry that one of them helped David escape. Think about the terrible nature of this act: Saul, the king over God's people, murders a group of men who are responsible for leading God's people in worship. The very one who is supposed to lead God's people according to God's word has become a source of violence, terror, and murder to them. This is an awful, bitter, sad, and devastating day for God's people. Even God's servants are not safe from this evil man.

Third, the passage concludes with one of the sons of Ahimelech, the priest who helped David, escaping from the brutal slaughter of Saul and coming to David in his "stronghold" (v. 4). There, David offers him "safekeeping" (v. 23), promising to protect his life along with the lives of all the other men who follow David. The passage ends in the way that it began—with a picture of the anointed king of God keeping outcasts safe and guarding their lives with his own. He is the true chosen one of God—the one who will not slaughter God's people but protect their lives.

What does this construction teach us? Obviously the shape of this passage is pointing to the drastic contrast between the reigning king—Saul—and God's anointed king—David. These two men could not be more different. Saul is slaughtering God's people, but David is protecting them and guarding their lives. The author of 1 Samuel is making this contrast on purpose to show the kind of king that David will be for God's people. Also, this passage is pointing forward to the ultimate anointed King of God—Jesus Christ himself. He is the one who will provide a safe place for misfits and outcasts as they repent of sin and turn to him as Savior and Lord. He will keep their souls safe for all eternity.

Psalm 51

The final practice text from Scripture that we'll consider is Psalm 51. It is a well-known psalm of David that has a very clear construction, which can be very helpful to us as we approach God in repentance. The context for this psalm is important (and this is a good reminder that our six hermeneutical tools work best when we use them together in our study of the Bible). David has just been confronted by the prophet Nathan because of his sin with Bathsheba and his murderous plot against Bathsheba's husband, Uriah. He recognizes his terrible sin and then writes this psalm—a prayer of confession and repentance—as his response.

READ!

Read Psalm 51 carefully and thoughtfully. It is a beautiful psalm of repentance, so focus on the words and King David's emotional, heartfelt confession of his sin. Also, though, focus on the construction of this psalm as you read. How is it put together? What are the different parts? How might those parts show the steps of repentance that David takes?

This psalm seems to break into four parts, with each part showing us a different step of repentance that David takes before God after being confronted with his sin. Here is how this works:

- *David begs for mercy and cleansing* (vv. 1–9). In this first section, David's focus is on confessing his sin fully and begging God to show him mercy and forgiveness. Every verse is full of honest acknowledgment of his sin, and also his need to be washed and cleansed by God's forgiving grace.
- *David asks for a clean heart* (vv. 10–12). Do you see how David's focus changes a bit in these verses? He is not simply asking God for mercy; he is asking God to get to the root of his sin and change his heart so that it will be cleaner and purer. He asks God to restore his "joy of your salvation" (v. 12)—a joy that will keep him from sinning in the first place.

- *David turns to teach others* (vv. 13–17). David's focus shifts again in these verses. He has confessed his sin and asked for forgiveness, and has also asked God to change his heart. Now he wants his experience of forgiveness and grace to lead him to "teach" (v. 13) others about God and the grace that can be found in him. David does not want his experience of God's grace to end with him; he wants it to be used for the benefit of other people.
- *David thinks about God's family* (vv. 18–19). In the final two verses, David gets even broader in his focus; he begins to think about the whole community of God's people. He asks God to "build up the walls" of his city (v. 18) and to delight in the sacrifices of his people (v. 19). David is recognizing, in other words, that his confession and repentance personally will be good for God's people communally. It is not just about him; he hopes that his confession and repentance will help the worship of God's people overall.

Do you see this clear structure? Do you see how these steps of repentance can help us understand the way we should approach God when we sin? How might you apply this passage to your life today as you bring sin to God, confess it, and ask for his forgiveness?

REVIEW

Congratulations on coming to the end of another chapter—and learning about and applying yet another tool for Bible study, interpretation, and application. You have learned about your fourth tool during this chapter, so now you have the context, courtroom, crux, and construction tools in your tool belts as you keep studying God's word.

You have two more tools to learn about in the next two chapters as you continue to grow in your capacity for handling God's word well in both interpretation and application. Hopefully you are feeling more and more equipped to study—and even teach—the Bible well.

Remember, the construction tool can help you find the structure (the shape or organization) of every biblical passage you study. This structure is the author's outline, and it is almost always the key to finding the author's emphasis and main point. Finding that point of emphasis can help protect you against focusing on the wrong things in a Bible passage or missing the correct application.

PRAY!

As you end this chapter with prayer, ask God to help you apply the construction tool in your study of his word moving forward. Pray that you would engage this tool not merely for academic purposes (although it is good to grow in your knowledge about the Bible), but also so that you can truly grasp the emphasis of every passage of Scripture that you study.

Chapter 6

THE CLARITY TOOL

The goal of the next tool that I want you to add to your hermeneutical tool belts—the clarity tool—is to help you let the Bible speak with utter clarity into your life—no matter what perspectives you naturally bring to Bible study. This tool is designed to serve as an important corrective and reminder that, in Bible study, the word of God must rule over our own perspectives, backgrounds, and agendas; we do not want any of our own opinions to color, infect, or distract from what the Bible is actually saying and teaching. Rather, we want the truth of the Bible to shine into our lives with *clarity*; we want to humbly allow God's word to speak for itself.

You'll note during the course of this chapter that there is significant interrelatedness between this tool and the context tool, which we covered in chapter 2. Often we find clarity on the main point of a biblical passage not only by identifying our own agendas and placing them to the side, but also by considering the wider context of what we're reading and studying. These tools are meant to be used together.

Remember, the clarity tool and the other tools we're studying in this book are not intended to help you do a full Bible study. Rather, they are general principles that help you approach Bible passages in the right way. The goal is to help you get the text right so that you can see the main point, as well as how that main point should relate to your life as you seek to follow and serve Jesus Christ.

Remember!

Your suggested memory verses for this chapter come from one of the passages we will consider with the help of the clarity tool later in this chapter.

Behold, I stand at the door and knock. If anyone hears my voice and opens the door, I will come in to him and eat with him, and he with me. The one who conquers, I will grant him to sit with me on my throne, as I also conquered and sat down with my Father on his throne. (Rev. 3:20–21)

UNDERSTANDING THIS TOOL

Every person has a perspective—a general outlook on life. These perspectives are not necessarily bad. In fact, you cannot help but have one. Our perspectives are made up of many factors; here are just a few:

- our upbringing
- our geographical location
- our ethnicity and appearance
- our family dynamics
- our political affiliations
- our church denomination
- our interests
- our tastes
- our gender

No matter where you live or where you come from, you cannot avoid having some kind of perspective for looking at the world. So it is good to think about the factors that make up your general outlook on life as you approach the Bible. No one who studies the Bible is able to completely leave his or her background behind; we all approach Bible study from within a certain human culture, living in a distinct geographical location, and at a particular point in world history.

However, Christians believe that the Bible is God's inspired word, given to human beings to help them know and worship him. So when we come to Scripture, we hope to hear God speak. No matter what perspectives or outlooks we bring to the biblical text, that is the goal—if we are serious about meeting God and knowing him through his revelation in Scripture. As best we can, we want to acknowledge the perspectives and backgrounds that we bring to the table in Bible study, but then discipline ourselves to not allow them to shape our interpretation and application of Scripture. The Bible sets the agenda; we must humbly allow it to do so.

The problem in Bible interpretation and application comes when we let our perspectives on life become bigger than the Bible itself. You see, the tendency for *all* of us is to read our perspectives into the Bible instead of letting the Bible rule over our outlooks and speak powerfully to us with authority and clarity. Every student of the Bible faces this temptation—and every one must battle against it.

This is exactly what the clarity tool is all about. The goal of this tool is to help us establish the principle that the Bible itself needs to be on the throne in our reading and study rather than our own perspectives. We need to let the Bible rule over what we often might want it to say. The clarity tool reminds us to be constantly guarding against reading our own desires into the text of Scripture so that we can be best prepared for God to speak with clarity into our lives through his inspired word. When we do this, as we'll see, the Bible often challenges our ways of thinking and our preferences.

In the coming pages, we are going to learn about some problems that come when this tool is not applied correctly, as well as some wonderful benefits that come when we allow the Bible, rather than our own perspectives, to rule our interpretation and application. Then, in the last part of this chapter, we will look at specific passages of Scripture that can illuminate the difference between letting the Bible rule and letting our own perspectives rule.

PROBLEMS AVOIDED WITH THIS TOOL

Various problems arise when the clarity tool is not properly used, with the result that people read their own perspectives into the Bible. Sometimes, as you will see, this is done intentionally; at other times, it is done innocently and ignorantly.

Here are just a few of the problems that can come when the clarity tool is not applied well:

False teaching. Perhaps the most obvious danger that comes from ignoring the clarity tool in the study and teaching of the Bible is false teaching. This is also the most intentional and pernicious problem. False teaching happens when people want to push their own false and ungodly perspectives. Instead of letting the Bible rule over them, they try to simply use it to back up false teaching. This is obviously a drastic and terrible example of not using the clarity tool. Scripture is abused when the selfish desire or agenda of an individual is lifted far above its truth and authority. One terrible and sad example of this from history is the way that some people actually tried to use the Bible to defend the practice of slavery. In another example, the "health-and-wealth gospel" is a rampant false teaching in many parts of the world today; it misuses passages about God's blessing for his people to teach that obedience to God will lead to physical health and material wealth. Such teachings are birthed from sinful human perspectives. Because these outlooks have become bigger than the clear teaching of God's word, they actually deny its truth.

Selective reading of Scripture. While false teaching is a very obvious problem that can come when the clarity tool is ignored and personal perspectives are pushed, there are also slightly less serious problems that originate from personal agendas. Sometimes Christians have perspectives that are not sinful—they want to motivate others to share the gospel, help people get involved in their communities, or encourage other believers to care for the poor. The problem comes when, in their zeal for their agendas, they rely on specific parts of the Bible rather than its whole teaching. When this happens, the Bible ceases to rule. Instead, their agendas actually start leading the way in how they interact with Scripture. We must be careful to not pick and choose Bible verses to support our own perspectives—even if we have good perspectives.

Right teaching from the wrong text. The most innocent problem that can result from failing to apply the clarity tool well is that people can teach *true* lessons about God (which are good) from texts of Scripture that do not actually proclaim those lessons. This usually happens from good motives; people want to understand and communicate a truth from the Bible that is really there somewhere. But they come to a text of the Bible hoping strongly to teach a certain truth about God, so they teach it whether or not that truth is actually in that passage. That is another way of failing to use the clarity tool; it is another way of refusing to let the Bible itself rule what is understood, taught, and applied.

If you are still feeling a bit unclear about this tool, that's OK. You will see how these problems can crop up as we go through practice texts from the Bible later in this chapter.

BENEFITS RECEIVED WITH THIS TOOL

Now let's seek to bring together some of the main benefits that come when we use the clarity tool well in our study of Scripture. The goal is to see the value of this tool so that you will be convinced that it should be used by everyone who seeks to understand and apply the Bible well. When Bible students let God's word rule, rather than their own perspectives, what is the result? When Bible teachers submit their own perspectives to the truth of the Scripture, what are the benefits?

Humility. First, when the clarity tool is put into practice carefully and diligently by Bible students and teachers, one important result is that it nurtures humility for people as they approach God's word. Their posture is not one of standing above the Bible, trying to shape it, form it, and use it to drive their own perspectives forward. Rather, their posture becomes one of humility—standing under the word and seeking to listen willingly to what it says. It is, in fact, simply impossible to put the clarity tool to work well without developing a certain amount of humility. Using this tool implies a conscious choice to humbly say, "What God has to say through his word is more important than what I would like to say." This is the right attitude to have in the study and interpretation of the Bible, because it humbly allows God to have the main agenda and the main voice in the conversation.

God's truth in all cultures. While no one, of course, is able to perfectly and totally leave every part of his or her perspective behind in the study of the Bible, the clarity tool helps people from many different cultures and mindsets gather around the authority of the word of the one true God of the universe. People from every kind of social, cultural, and ethnic background can place themselves under the rule of the Bible and seek to leave their own perspectives at the door as they turn to study, interpret, and apply God's word together. This is difficult work. Yet the clarity tool reminds us that Christians are called to let the Bible be the supreme voice in the conversation between God's people, even when they come from many different cultures.

Protection for God's people. Finally, the clarity tool, when used well by Bible teachers, pastors, and others who communicate God's word to God's people, can be an important form of protection for God's people. When those who teach the Bible humbly submit to the rule of God's word rather than their own perspectives and agendas, they are protecting the people they teach from simply hearing the opinions and preferences of mere men and women. Using the clarity tool, then, is a way to guard people and help them hear from the Bible first rather than from the mouths of humans who are trying to get them to act in certain ways.

APPLYING THIS TOOL

Let's now put the clarity tool to work in the study of several Bible passages. In each of these application examples, you will first read the passage, then identify the mistakes that people might make by failing to use the clarity tool, and finally seek to interpret the verse or passage faithfully by putting the tool to work. I hope these examples will give you good practice in bringing clarity into your study of every part of the Bible.

Mark 4:35–41

I hope you now feel that you have a good grasp of the clarity tool. We have defined and described it; we have discussed the problems that come from failing to put it to work; and we have identified the main benefits of using it well. It really is an incredibly important tool because, as we noted above, it has to do with our posture before God's word. Will we stand over the Bible, letting our own perspectives rule our interpretation, understanding, and application of it? Or will we stand under God's word, letting its authority shape our lives and humbly submitting to what God says rather than what we might want him to say?

We'll begin practicing how to put this tool to work by looking at Mark 4:35–41. You are going to see how, when a certain perspective rules over this text, the Bible can seem to say something very different than what God actually is saying through the passage. We will see, by way of contrast, the importance of letting God's word itself speak more loudly then our own perspectives, agendas, and desires.

READ!

Read Mark 4:35–41 carefully, slowly, and thoughtfully. It is a short passage, so read it through at least twice. Think about the main point that this passage is teaching us as followers of Jesus Christ. Imagine that you are bringing a comfort *perspective to your study of this biblical text (you want to use this passage to encourage someone who's going through a tough time). How might you use this passage if you were bringing that agenda to it?*

If we were to let a *comfort* perspective rule over our interpretation and application of this text, we would probably tell hurting or struggling people that this is a passage about Jesus solving their problems, helping them, and making their struggles go away. We might see the great literal storm in this passage as a picture of the figurative storms that often come into our lives—our problems, struggles, frustrations, and trials. Thus, Jesus is the one who calms our storms; that is, he makes our problems go away. You see, when comfort is the perspective that rules our approach, that is likely to be the message that we take from this passage in the Gospel of Mark.

Yet when we use the clarity tool and actually allow the text of Scripture to rule our interpretation and application, we begin to see that this passage from Mark is actually not about comfort at all. How do we know this?

All we have to do is to look at verse 41. After Jesus calms the storm in the presence of his disciples, what is their response? Are they comforted? Do they feel "all better" now that Jesus has taken the storm away? Absolutely not; in fact, they are "filled with great fear" because of what they have just seen Jesus do. In other words, they are now much more frightened of Jesus—his great authority, power, and glory—than they had been of the storm that had threatened their very lives. The disciples have moved not from fear to comfort in this passage, but from fear to deeper fear.

When we let this passage speak for itself (that is, using the clarity tool), we find that it is not about *comfort* but about being *confronted* with the power, authority, and glory of Jesus Christ as the Son of God. Jesus is the one who can calm a storm with a word; our greatest problem is figuring out how we will respond to this amazing God. Will we put our faith in him and obey him, just as the wind and the waves did? The eternal weight of that question is greater than the earthly storms we face in our lives.

From this example, you can see the importance of letting the text of the Bible speak rather than any of our own perspectives that we might try to bring to the text. We need to sit under God's word and let it say to us what God wants to say.

Before we move on to our next passage, consider these questions:

- Is the perspective of comfort (or the desire to use Scripture to comfort another person) a bad perspective or motivation?
- Are there passages in the Bible that talk about comfort for God's people? Which ones can you think of?

I hope you answered no to the first question and yes to the second one (and that you thought of a few biblical passages that are aimed at comforting the people of God). The point of our engagement with Mark 4:35–41 was not to teach you that comfort is never the goal of any passage in Scripture. The point was to show you that even a good perspective (like comfort) should never be brought to a text of Scripture in a way that makes it bigger than God's word. We should always let the Bible rule and speak to us rather than a certain perspective or agenda. That is precisely what the clarity tool is all about.

Revelation 3:20

Let's look now at another passage: Revelation 3:20 (we looked at Jesus's tone in this passage in chap. 2). Here you are going to see how another good perspective—in this case, *evangelistic witness*—should not get in the way of allowing the actual text of Scripture to speak to us.

READ!

Read Revelation 3:20 (one of your suggested memory verses for this chapter). Think about how an evangelistic-witness agenda might lead you to read, interpret, and apply this verse. Then read the surrounding verses—the entire message from Jesus to the church at Laodicea (vv. 14–22). Think about the message that the text itself is speaking to God's people there—and today.

The Bible, in many places, calls us to share the gospel and to invite others to believe in Jesus. But what is *this* passage in Revelation 3 talking about? What is the main point *here*? How should we apply the clarity tool to this passage in order to allow Scripture to set the agenda and rule over us as we humbly submit to God's word?

When you imagined adopting an evangelistic-witness perspective, how did you read Revelation 3:20? You probably read it as the words of a meek and mild Jesus gently knocking on the doors of peoples' hearts, asking them for permission to come into their lives. His tone, then, is kind, calm, and quiet.

Under this perspective, who is the immediate audience for Jesus's words in this passage? It is unbelievers—people who have not yet decided to follow him or be part of his church. You see, when an evangelism agenda rules over this text, these verses take on the meaning of evangelism: Jesus is making a gentle appeal to people who have not yet decided to follow him, asking them to invite him into their hearts.

When you left that perspective at the door and looked at the broader text (vv. 14–22), allowing it to rule, what did you see? You saw that the appeal from Jesus in verse 20 is set in the context of a brutal and stern *rebuke* to the *church* of Laodicea. Jesus has actually just called these believers "wretched, pitiable, poor, blind, and naked" (v. 17)! He has said that, because of the way they are acting and functioning spiritually, he is about to "spit" (or "vomit") them out of his mouth (v. 16). Jesus is angry with the Laodiceans because they are spiritually proud and have come to a point where they do not think they need him or his grace. He therefore calls them to repentance, telling them that they need to find forgiveness and cleansing from him.

So when we let this text be king, we see that Jesus's tone is not a gentle and mild invitation but a stern rebuke. We also see that his audience is not people who do not know him (unbelievers), but people who claim to be following him (professing believers who belong to the church). This passage is a wake-up call for the church, not an evangelistic appeal to those outside the church.

As I mentioned above, many passages in Scripture can be used to call people to Jesus with gentle and inviting words. This passage is simply not one of them. This is clear when we put the clarity tool to work in Revelation 3.

Romans 8:31–39

In the past two Scripture examples, we have looked at perspectives or agendas that are generally good. The perspective of comfort is not bad; it simply is not the main focus of Mark 4:35–41. Likewise, the perspective of evangelistic witness is certainly found throughout Scripture; it just is not in Revelation 3:14–22. The goal of those biblical examples was to demonstrate the importance of the clarity tool in Bible interpretation and application. As students of God's word, we do not want even good perspectives or agendas to dominate the way we sit under the Bible. We want to study it and hear clearly what God has to say to us, leaving our unique perspectives at the door as much as possible.

In our next example, though, we are going to turn to a perspective that is a bit more problematic, and even—in some cases—sinful. That perspective is sometimes referred to as *health-and-wealth teaching* or the prosperity gospel. The general thrust of this agenda is an understanding that true faith in Jesus will lead to a victorious and successful life, one filled with prosperity (and often physical health and healing too). This idea is not taught in Scripture, but it can sometimes be forced onto certain texts of the Bible, as we will see in this section.

READ!

Read Romans 8:31–39 carefully and thoughtfully, considering the ways that a health-and-wealth agenda might seek to shape this passage to fit that perspective. Look out also for verses in this passage that might prove that it is not *teaching a prosperity gospel.*

If we were to come to Romans 8:31–39 with a health-and-wealth perspective, how might we interpret and apply this passage?

We might look at verse 32 and see a promise that God is going to give us everything we want: "He who did not spare his own Son but gave him up for us all, how will he not also with him graciously give us all things?" We might link that to material blessings—money, possessions, or career success. We might pick up the phrase "more than conquerors" from verse 37 and make that a kind of motto for victorious living through Jesus Christ. We might conclude that this verse is declaring that we can conquer any hardship, situation, or conflict and come out victorious, wealthy, and successful. If our minds are already moving in a health-and-wealth direction when we read this passage, it's easy to find some verses that seem to back up our suspicion that God has massive earthly success, glory, and comfort in store for us.

But what do you see when you look more closely at the passage? When you let the text rule rather than a health-and-wealth perspective, what sticks out to you? You probably notice that verse 36 does not quite fit the prosperity agenda. Paul quotes from the Old Testament as he describes the experience of followers of Jesus Christ: "For your sake we are being killed all the day long; we are regarded as sheep to be slaughtered." So Paul actually is talking about the love of Christ for believers in the context of *suffering*; some of them are even being killed!

When we look back a few verses, we see that this passage is set in the context of "groaning" (v. 22). The world groans as it waits for Christ to make all things new, and we, too, groan as we wait for the glory of our Savior in the new heaven and new earth. In other words, there *will be* health and wealth for followers of Jesus Christ, but not ultimately on this earth. Our hope is in the eternal glory that we have in Jesus Christ, and that may come after great suffering and hardship as we follow him here on earth. The promise for God's people who trust Jesus Christ is not earthly health and wealth; it's eternal heavenly blessing in the presence of Jesus.

We should think here, too, about the example of our Lord Jesus Christ. His life was *not* a health-and-wealth experience. He suffered and died on a cross to rescue guilty people from their sin. He called his followers to take up the cross and follow him. We should be ready to follow Jesus in any circumstance, but we should never expect that faithfulness to him will always result in wealth, prosperity, and comfort. If anything, we should expect suffering in this life as we follow the path of our Lord and Savior, who suffered in our place.

1 Samuel 17

Sometimes the clarity tool is helpful for avoiding confusion during Bible study by keeping us focused on the main point of the passage. However, in some cases, it can actually protect us from thinking that a passage in Scripture says the exact opposite of what it is saying. We just saw how this was true with Romans 8:31–39, and we're going to see it demonstrated again in the next passage we will study—1 Samuel 17. This is one of the most well-known passages in all of the Bible, for it is here that we find the story of David and Goliath. Let's think about how the clarity tool can help us let the text of this passage speak to us in such a way that we can see the main point.

READ!

First Samuel 17 is a long passage, but it is important that you read this entire account of the battle of David and Goliath. As you read, think about ways that people with an individual-motivation perspective might understand this passage. When we identify with David, the hero of the story, how do we tend to interpret and apply this familiar portion of Scripture?

As with the previous passages we've considered, this passage can be interpreted and applied in two general ways—one in which an outside perspective rules, and one in which the text itself is allowed to rule.

First, think about this passage from an *individual-motivation* perspective, which causes you (the reader) to identify yourself with David, the hero. How would you interpret and apply this passage from that perspective? What might be some of your main takeaways from your study of this biblical text?

You would see that David, although he is just a young boy, is completely unafraid of a giant—Goliath—who is a great enemy of God's people. You would see how David goes boldly into battle and defeats Goliath—a man much larger and physically stronger than himself. Then you would begin to make applications about courage, strength, boldness, and being the underdog in a situation, trial, or challenge. In short, you would use this passage to motivate yourself to be like David as you persevere and fight seemingly insurmountable odds in life, work, or other situations. This passage would become a moral lesson or pep talk about becoming a "giant killer" as you imitate David and defeat your challenges and problems.

Now look at the passage again. When we let the passage rule, we find that the individual-motivation perspective may not yield the correct interpretation and application. Why is it not quite right for us, as God's people today, to identify ourselves first with David?

Look at verse 11. How are all the men of Israel's army—including King Saul—responding to Goliath's threats? They are terrified of this giant, intimidating man. They do not know what to do. This is not a very good look for the soldiers of the army of the people of God.

Now glance back at 1 Samuel 16 to get some of the context that leads into this chapter. Here, David is anointed by Samuel as the next king of Israel. So David is God's chosen savior and ruler for his people (the people who, in chapter 17, are cowering in fear at the sight of their giant enemy).

Do you see where we are going with this? With whom, actually, is the text telling us we should identify? We should not be identifying with David; there's only one of him, and he's just been uniquely anointed by God. We're supposed to identify ourselves with the people of God. They are helpless in the face of their enemies, but God is at work raising up a great hero who will be able to save them.

So when we let the text itself rule rather than our perspective, we begin to see that the story of David and Goliath is not about motivating us to courageous action and accomplishment (as we try to be like David); rather, it is a hint to us of what God's great King—Jesus—will do for helpless people who need rescue from sin, Satan, and death—the greatest enemies of God's people. God is in the business of raising up a representative warrior who will fight the enemies of his people on their behalf in order to save and deliver them. David, then, is a picture of Jesus as he saves God's helpless people from the giant Goliath. He is the representative warrior for helpless people, just as Jesus is our representative Savior. Therefore, this passage is an encouragement for us to look to Jesus—the ultimate David.

2 Corinthians 9:6–15

Another passage that can easily be misunderstood is 2 Corinthians 9:6–15, especially if people from churches come to it with a certain perspective or outlook. As we continue practicing how to study Scripture with the clarity tool, we will adopt the agenda of *giving to the church* as we consider this passage. This perspective may not be something that you think about very often. Yet many local churches are supported and sustained by the gifts, tithes, and offerings of their members. Giving to one's local church is a very important part of Christian faith and worship; you should begin thinking, even now, about how giving to your church can be a part of the way you generously support the advance of the gospel and worship God with your money. However, when we bring the perspective of giving to the church to a passage like 2 Corinthians 9:6–15 and allow it to rule over the text, we can get ourselves into serious trouble. Let's find out what this looks like.

READ!

Read 2 Corinthians 9:6–15 carefully and begin thinking about how it might be understood from the perspective of giving to the church. Then take a look at verses 1–5. How do these verses help correct this perspective as you study verses 6–15?

How might we use this passage if we were church leaders trying to encourage our congregations to give? We might be tempted to use the teaching in verses 6–9 to talk about the right attitude we should have in giving; we would encourage people that it is good for them to give with cheerful and joyful hearts. Then we might encourage them with the words of verse 10—that God will "increase the harvest" of their giving and use their generosity to do wonderful things for the gospel. We might end with a strong call for them to give tithes and offerings to the local church; we could even attach it to a big building campaign.

All in all, we would be focusing on the text itself, but we would be missing a very important point about this passage: while it is about giving, it is not necessarily about giving to the local church. How do we know this?

When we put the clarity tool to work and look carefully at what is happening in this passage, we begin to see that the context here is not Paul encouraging Corinthian believers to give to the church of Corinth. So if church leaders are really going to let this text rule, they cannot use it to tell Christians that they have to give to their local churches (although other passages in the Bible certainly offer principles that move believers in that direction).

What is the context of the commands and instructions regarding generosity in this passage? The context is a collection for the saints in Jerusalem—far away from Corinth. Paul is encouraging the believers in Corinth to give generously to help needy Christians *in other places*—not simply to support the work of the Corinthian church. If anything, the call to generosity in this passage is a call to mercy ministry, a call to help believers in other parts of the world who are enduring hardships, trials, or crisis situations.

So is it good to give generously to your local church? Of course. But church leaders should always be careful not to use Bible passages to say things that they actually do not say. When we put the clarity tool to work in this passage and allow the text to rule, we see that the call to generosity in 2 Corinthians 9 is a call to help Christians in need in other places.

Colossians 4:2–6

You have now put the clarity tool to work in several passages of Scripture. Hopefully you have seen how the principle behind this tool—that the text, not our own perspectives, must rule as we study the Bible—is incredibly important for the right understanding and application of God's word.

In the final example we'll consider, Paul speaks to the people in the church at Colossae, many of whom probably have regular jobs in the working world of their day. What he says to them is focused on their gospel witness, but not only on *their* gospel witness. Our goal, as in all of the passages we've studied, is to let the text speak and rule as we see what it says.

READ!

Read Colossians 4:2–6. It is a brief passage, so read it through at least two times. Think about adopting a perspective of sharing the gospel at work *for this passage, an outlook specifically geared toward people who work in the professional world. How might that agenda influence the way you would understand and apply this passage?*

If we were to adopt a perspective of sharing the gospel at work for this text, we might be tempted to skip over verses 2–4 of the passage and move to an emphasis on verses 5–6. We would probably focus especially on verse 5 and call people to make "the best use of the time" at work in sharing the gospel with the people around them. We would urge people to let their speech be "seasoned" (v. 6) with the salt of the gospel and tell them to always be talking about Jesus to people who do not yet know him. If we are not careful, we might even put unnecessary guilt on people who are not actively sharing their faith in their offices as they also try to get their work done in a good way.

How does this emphasis depart from the point that Paul is making in this passage? When we put the clarity tool to work in this passage, we see that Paul's first emphasis is actually on the Colossians' prayer for *his* ministry and the ministry of the apostles (vv. 3–4). So first they are called to pray that the gospel would continue to go forth through Paul's preaching. Then, in verse 5, Paul calls them to be wise toward "outsiders." This certainly means doing good work in the business world and being good employees. Finally, verse 6 reminds them to stand ready to "answer each person" about the truth of the gospel. What does all this mean?

While sharing the gospel should be a regular part of the life of every Christian, Paul is not necessarily saying that people who work in the professional world need to be trying to preach the gospel every minute as they do their jobs. In fact, part of walking "in wisdom toward outsiders" (v. 5) is surely being a good employee: focusing on one's job with diligence and hard work, without laziness or yielding to distractions. There may be times to share the gospel in the workplace, but Christians should also be good workers.

In this passage, Paul is calling people to pray for the advance of the gospel through the ministry of the apostles (carried on today through the local church, which proclaims the apostolic gospel), to act wisely toward people who do not know Jesus, and to always stand ready to answer questions about Jesus and the gospel. This focus becomes clear to us when we put the clarity tool to work as we study this text.

REVIEW

Congratulations on coming to the end of another chapter. You've learned about the clarity tool and its importance for the right interpretation and application of Scripture. The sad reality is that many people today import their own perspectives into Bible study and allow them to rule over God's word as they interpret and apply it. The clarity tool reminds us that the Bible itself must rule; our goal is to sit under its authority and do everything we can to let it speak clearly and powerfully to our lives. Doing so protects us against false teaching, personal agendas, and misunderstandings of the emphasis of passages in the Bible. Furthermore, using the clarity tool promotes humility on our part because it requires us to put aside our own agendas and perspectives to sit under God's word.

PRAY!

As you end this chapter on the clarity tool, pray that God would help you apply the principle behind this tool in your study of his word in the days to come. Ask him to protect you from letting your own perspectives, agendas, and outlooks influence the way you interpret and apply the Bible. Pray that he would give you the humility that you need to sit willingly under his word, looking to him alone for illumination and instruction.

Chapter 7

THE CROSS TOOL

Far too often, Bible students seek to understand and apply Scripture without considering that the death and resurrection of Jesus Christ—the message of the gospel—is the very center of the Scriptures. To guard you from making this mistake in your own study of the Bible, I want to introduce you in this chapter to the last tool for your hermeneutical tool belts—the cross tool.

Throughout this book, we've seen that these tools that you are learning about are not designed to do *all* the work of Bible study for you. Rather, they are general principles that can help you stay on track as you seek to interpret and apply the Bible well. The cross tool may be the most important principle for getting into God's word, understanding it rightly, and applying it faithfully to our lives today. We should always seek a *gospel-centered* interpretation and application of the Bible, specifically one that takes into account the central message and climax of the Bible—the person and work of Jesus Christ. It is no exaggeration to say that if we miss the gospel in our Bible reading and study, we have missed everything. As in the earlier chapters, we'll begin with an explanatory introduction to the cross tool, look at some problems it helps us avoid and some benefits it confers, and then seek to apply it in a few practice texts.

Remember!

Your memory verses for this chapter come from the very end of Luke's Gospel, as he recounts what Jesus taught his disciples about understanding the Bible. Think about the importance and significance of this teaching for Bible study. Jesus is linking his work and salvation with the message of the entire Bible.

Then he said to them, "These are my words that I spoke to you while I was still with you, that everything written about me in the Law of Moses and the Prophets and the Psalms must be fulfilled." Then he opened their minds to understand the Scriptures, and said to them, "Thus it is written, that the Christ should suffer and on the third day rise from the dead, and that repentance for the forgiveness of sins should be proclaimed in his name to all nations, beginning from Jerusalem." (Luke 24:44–47)

UNDERSTANDING THIS TOOL

Very often, using the cross tool involves asking, "How does this passage connect to the cross of Jesus Christ (as well as his incarnation, faithful life of obedience, resurrection, and future reign)?" In other words, it is all about the centrality of the gospel in the Bible—and therefore in your study of the Bible.

What is the gospel? From 1 Corinthians 15:1–4, among other passages in the Bible, we see that the gospel is *the good news that Jesus Christ, God's Son, died for sins and rose from the dead in order to save God's people, and that all of this fulfilled the Scriptures of the Old Testament.* It is good to remember the part about the Old Testament because Paul focuses on it in a very strong way, writing "in accordance with the Scriptures" twice in these verses (vv. 3, 4). This means that all of the Bible is about the gospel; the whole Old Testament points ahead to the saving work of Jesus through his death on the cross and his resurrection from the dead. This salvation that Jesus offers is received only by faith, as we see in the New Testament. So the gospel is a proclamation of the good news about what God, in Christ, has done for sinners, who can then receive the gospel through repentance and faith in Jesus.

Jesus himself reminds us that it is good and legitimate for us to use the cross tool in our Bible study—even our study of the Old Testament. In Luke 24:27, we read about a sermon that Jesus preaches to two disciples on the road to Emmaus, explaining to them from the entire Old Testament all the things "concerning himself." Also, in John 5:39, Jesus tells the Pharisees that the Old Testament Scriptures testify about him. As Jesus, the very Son of God, interacts with the Bible, he uses the cross tool, showing that everything is ultimately pointing to the great salvation that he will provide for God's people through his death and resurrection. Jesus interprets all of Scripture with reference to himself.

Since all of this is true, it would be foolish for us, in our study of any part of Scripture, to fail to go through the cross in our interpretation and application. If the gospel really is the point of the Bible, and it all comes to a climax in the death and resurrection of Jesus Christ, then we need to work hard to see how every part of the story points to him. In our Bible study, we must get to Christ. This is the principle behind the cross tool.

PROBLEMS AVOIDED WITH THIS TOOL

The sad reality is that many people, even people who love the Bible, simply do not see that Jesus's salvation is the climax of God's great story and that the gospel really is central to the message of Scripture. By failing to use the cross tool, they miss the power of the gospel in the way they read and study the Bible. This can lead to all kinds of problems, including the following:

Moralism/legalism. Moralism and legalism are, by far, the most common problems that can come through Bible study that does not include an intentional effort to put the cross tool to work. If we do not see the gospel as central to the Bible and discipline ourselves to run to it in our study of every part of God's word, we are going to tend to default to moralistic lessons that only result in legalism.

What do I mean by moralism and legalism? Moralism is merely trying to be good without seeing that true goodness is found only in God, who gives grace through Jesus to sinners who can never be good on their own. Legalism is the keeping of rules in the hope of earning God's favor rather than seeing that God's favor has been poured out on those who put their faith and trust in Jesus Christ, who alone can earn God's favor for sinners. Without the cross tool, many passages in Scripture will be understood and applied simply as rules for life; they will be applied moralistically, without consideration of the miraculous work of the Holy Spirit in our hearts as we receive the gospel of Jesus Christ.

Guilt with no grace. Moralism and legalism lead to this second problem: guilt with no grace. When our application from passages of Scripture is essentially "Do more and be better" again and again, we only heap guilt on people rather than exposing them to God's amazing grace that is shown most beautifully to us at the cross of Jesus Christ. Since the Bible really does point to the death and resurrection of Jesus Christ in every part (Jesus says it does), to ignore the gospel as we tell people to "shape up and act right" is actually an abuse of the very word of God because it is missing the crucial climax.

A wrong view of the Bible. Finally, to miss the cross tool is to have a wrong view of the Bible. If we take Jesus's words seriously (that the Law, the Prophets, and the Psalms speak of him), then to understand the Bible rightly, we need to see that every part of it points to him. This relates to our view of God's inspiration of the Bible as well. Since God is the divine author of Scripture, it makes sense that the Bible tells one unified story that centers on the gospel of his Son. To miss that gospel in various parts of this story is to ignore the fact that God is intentionally weaving it all together to show us his Son.

This means that utilizing the cross tool in our study of the Scriptures affirms the unity of the Bible—that it tells a unified story of God's work of creation, redemption, and ultimately restoration in a world (and a people) marred by sin. Because the Bible is God's story—and the person and work of Jesus is the climax of that story—every part of the story is rightly read, studied, understood, and applied with reference to the climax.

BENEFITS RECEIVED WITH THIS TOOL

Now let's shift our attention to the main benefits that come when we commit to applying the cross tool to our study of the Bible. When we put this tool to work, we can be sure that we will do the following:

Read the Bible as one story. The main problem that many people have in Bible study is that they simply do not see how the many parts of the Bible are connected as one story. As a result, they miss the way that different parts of the story point to the ultimate climax in Jesus Christ and the salvation that he brings to God's people. Asking how every passage of the Bible relates to the gospel reminds us to study the Scriptures as one story. God was the author, inspiring human authors to write and telling one big story of his gracious, powerful, and saving work in the world. This work culminated in the life, death, resurrection, and ascension of his own Son. The cross tool helps us come back again and again to the fact that the Bible really is telling this one big story of God's salvation in the world.

Read the Bible as Jesus did. I have mentioned this before, but it is worth saying again: Jesus used the cross tool as he interacted with the Old Testament Scriptures. He did not see the Old Testament as an unrelated account of God's work in the world, but as the witness of God that pointed to his climactic saving work through his death and resurrection.

Jesus explains this to his disciples in the passage from Luke 24 that we referenced earlier (and which I encourage you to memorize as you work through this chapter). He demonstrates this as he quotes from the Old Testament as he hangs on the cross. Again and again he teaches this to his disciples, and even to the Pharisees. Jesus sees the Bible as a story that is ultimately about him. So should we, his followers.

Read the Bible and find grace. This benefit is the other side of the tendency to descend into moralism and legalism as we study the Bible. When we put the cross tool to work in our study of God's word, we are protected from a "Do more and be better" kind of application in our study. We begin to see that the gospel must be central at each point. We understand that every part of the Bible is pointing us to God's final salvation, which is fully demonstrated on a cross, where his own Son offered himself as the final sacrifice for sinners who could never save themselves. The saving grace of God, received by faith, is the only source and power for true change in people's lives, as the Holy Spirit indwells us and enables our obedience and growth in holiness. The message of the Bible is not "Do more and be better," but rather "Look to the cross to see what Jesus *did* there for you, and believe in him, follow him, and learn to obey him."

APPLYING THIS TOOL

We're almost ready to actually put the cross tool to work in specific passages of the Bible. But before we do that, I want to give you a few more detailed instructions about how you can learn to use this tool. It is one thing to know, in principle, that we must see how any passage relates to the gospel, but it is another thing completely to actually see how to get to the gospel from any passage. So let me suggest a few paths that you can take to travel to the cross of Christ from Old Testament passages.

Typology. One way that we see the gospel in the Old Testament is through something called typology. This happens when God uses an

Old Testament character in a powerful saving or leading way for his people. This person becomes a type—or a picture—of Jesus and all that he will accomplish for God's people. Samuel, for example, is a prophet for God's people as he speaks God's word to them; a priest as he intercedes and makes sacrifices for them; and a judge, or kingly figure, as he rules and leads them. In this way, he is a type of Christ, who will come later as the perfect Prophet, Priest, and King of God's people.

Patterns. Sometimes, the Old Testament shows us patterns of the way God works in the lives of his people. We saw this, for example, in the story of David and Goliath from 1 Samuel 17. God gives his people a pattern of how he will work on their behalf as he raises up a savior (the anointed king, David) who does battle with their great enemy, Goliath, on their behalf. This is a pattern of the much greater salvation that God will one day offer through his perfect anointed King, Jesus. Such patterns are repeated—in bigger and bigger ways—until they break forth in beautiful fulfillments through the person and work of Jesus Christ.

Need. Some sad passages in the Old Testament simply show us the sin and rebellion of God's people in order to highlight the great need for a Savior who can deliver his people from sin forever. Passages from Judges show us the sin of God's people in very obvious ways. Many of the prophets also highlight the rebellion and stubbornness of God's people, revealing the need for a Messiah who will come and finally offer them salvation, grace, and forgiveness. Even the sinful failure of King David reveals a great need—for a perfect King, who will never fail, to reign over God's people.

Prophecy/promise. Sometimes the Old Testament makes it easy on us. There are, of course, specific prophecies that point very directly to the coming reign and salvation of Jesus Christ, as well as promises that can be fulfilled only through the coming of a divine King like Jesus. Genesis 3:15 points us to the final victory over Satan by the "offspring" of Eve. Isaiah 53:11 speaks of a suffering "servant" who will come to pay for the sins of God's people. Micah 5:2 tells us that the Messiah will be born in Bethlehem. In Deuteronomy 18:15, Moses speaks of a prophet like him who will come one day to lead God's people. In 2 Samuel 7:12–13, God promises David that his "offspring" will rule the kingdom forever. All of these prophecies and promises point to the eternal reign of a divine King and ruler over God's people.

With that background in place, let's now put the cross tool to work in the study of several Bible passages. In each example, you will begin by reading an Old Testament passage, then think about what our interpretation and application might look like without using the cross tool, and end by seeking to interpret and apply the verse or passage faithfully by putting the tool to work. The goal is to give you good practice at finding your way to the gospel of Christ from any part of the Bible.

Joshua 5:13–15

We'll start with Joshua 5:13–15. This is the account of an interaction between Joshua, the great leader of God's people, and the "commander of the army of the Lord" (v. 14) just before Joshua leads God's people to a great victory against the city of Jericho. As you study this passage now, you are going to see how we might be tempted to ignore the cross tool and skip the gospel in the way we interpret and apply this text. You also will see the richer meaning and application we discover when we use this tool.

READ!

Read through Joshua 5:13–15 slowly and carefully at least twice. As you read, begin thinking about what is happening here and how it relates to the gospel of Jesus Christ. What are some ways that we might miss the gospel as we read and study this passage?

Before we apply the cross tool to this passage, let's think about what will happen if we *fail* to do so. How will we interpret and apply the passage if we never make it to the gospel?

We will see that Joshua, the commander of God's people, has a confrontation with either an angel of God or God himself (some people think this is an appearance of Jesus). Obviously, this heavenly "commander" (Josh. 5:14) is reminding Joshua of who is truly in charge. Joshua is ready to do battle against his enemies, but he needs to be reminded that, in order to lead God's people well, he needs to *be* led by God as he worships the true King and commander. This is, indeed, a good reminder for anyone in leadership. If we want to lead others well, we need to make sure that we are following God.

However, if we stop there in our interpretation and application of this passage, we have not quite made it to the gospel. We have not fully put the cross tool to work. So how do we use this tool in Joshua 5?

We need to see the *why* behind this confrontation between Joshua and the heavenly commander. You see, Joshua is an amazing leader for God's people. He is a mighty warrior, a word-centered leader, and a very faithful king of sorts to the Israelites. In fact, his name is even related to the name Jesus! Yet we see from this passage that even this great and mighty leader for God's people is not holy enough to stand in the presence of God, for he needs to remove his shoes. This means he is not worthy to be the true "Jesus" for God's people. God will use him, but he is not the final answer for the people's sin problem. As wonderful as Joshua is, he points us to a future leader who will be as holy as God himself; one who will be God in human flesh. In other words, even this great Joshua, the savior of God's people, needs a Savior himself. And all of God's sinful people need to be led by the greater Joshua—Jesus, who is perfectly holy and perfectly good.

Judges 2:6–15

Now we are going to move forward one book in the Bible and look at a passage from the book of Judges. This passage from chapter 2 records the death of Joshua, whom we have just read about. As you study this passage now, you are going to consider how the cross tool can—and should—be put to work in this text too. The goal is not only to make true statements about the text, but also to see how this passage relates to the gospel of Jesus Christ.

READ!

Take some time to read Judges 2:6–15 carefully. Begin thinking about how the cross tool might help you interpret and apply this passage in a gospel-centered way. Here is a hint: What problem is this passage identifying in the lives of God's people?

Once again, let's think about the truth that this passage is teaching without putting the cross tool to work yet. What is going on in this passage, and how will we summarize and apply it without actively moving toward the gospel?

We can see that God's people are struggling to obey him without the good leadership of Joshua. After Joshua dies, the people who rise up in the next generation do not fear God and do not worship him alone. They abandon God (v. 12) and turn to the worship of idols. So God gives them into the hands of their enemies. They are conquered by other peoples and come under "terrible distress" (v. 15) because of their sin.

If we focus on just these basic facts about this passage without putting the cross tool to work, we will probably summarize it this way: God's people, without a good leader, fall into sin and idolatry, and they pay for it in terrible ways. That summary correctly identifies the main point of this passage, in one sense; it *is* showing us the sinfulness of God's people and the devastating results that sin brings into their lives. It is also making a connection to leadership, since this all happens after the death of the great leader Joshua. But what have we missed here? What difference will the cross tool make for our reading of this passage?

When we bring the cross tool into our study and remember that the gospel is the very center of the Bible, we begin to see that this passage highlights the disobedience of God's people in order to show us their great need for a leader who will be able to finally deal with their sin.

Without Joshua, they are hopeless and rebellious, and they descend into the foolish and terrible worship of idols. Even when God begins to raise up judges, the people still fail, again and again, to stick with God in faithful worship and obedience. God's people need someone to help them stay faithful to God. Joshua was not that someone, and no judge is able to fulfill this role perfectly either.

An Old Testament passage like this is meant to drive us to the cross—the place where, one day, God will allow his own Son to pay the penalty for the sins of his people and lead them in obedience, right worship, and holiness through the Holy Spirit. Jesus's sacrificial death is the only way that their sin can finally be dealt with—and he is the only leader who can guide them into obedience and an ongoing right relationship with the holy God.

1 Samuel 13:1–14

Are you beginning to see how the cross tool makes a difference in your study of God's word? Are you coming to understand the value of gospel-centered interpretation and application of Scripture?

Let's continue moving forward through the Bible to 1 Samuel 13. This passage focuses on King Saul, who ultimately failed miserably to lead God's people in a godly, faithful, and obedient way. As you study this passage with the cross tool, the goal is for you to see how a gospel-centered application leads us toward the only true path of faithful obedience, for Saul's failure ultimately points us to the worthiness of King Jesus and the call to repent of our sins and follow and obey him.

READ!

Read 1 Samuel 13:1–14 carefully and thoughtfully. As you read, think about the way this passage shows us the failure of King Saul. How does he fail? How might this failure point us to the success of King Jesus?

This is a very sad passage. God's people are being defeated by the Philistines, and things are so bad that many of them are hiding in caves and among rocks just to escape this vicious enemy. In the midst of this, Saul is waiting for Samuel, who has promised to come and make a sacrifice for the people before they continue in battle. Samuel, after all, is the priest for God's people. According to God's law, Saul cannot act as both a priest and a king; this is why he is supposed to wait for Samuel to make the sacrifice. But as you read in the passage, Saul does not wait for Samuel. Instead, he offers a sacrifice himself, acting as a priest for God's people even though he is not supposed to. Because of this act of disobedience, God rejects him as king.

If we do not use the cross tool as we study this passage, we will probably focus on Saul's failure and simply stop there. We will see that this king fails to obey, so he is rejected by Samuel and by God. In our application of this passage, we might stress the importance of obeying God's word. We will see Saul as an example to us of how we should listen carefully to God, be faithful to him, and do what he says.

But if we merely focus on obedience, we will be making only a *moralistic* application from this passage. Do you remember that word, which we considered earlier? By making such an application, we will be telling ourselves to be better people, but we will not have actually moved toward the gospel from this Old Testament passage.

So how do we do that? How do we use the cross tool to avoid simply teaching a moral lesson that doesn't get to Jesus and the cross at all?

One way that we might do this is to see that Saul is a king who tried to act as a priest, but was rejected because he was sinful and therefore not worthy to fulfill both of those functions for God's people. Saul's disobedience disqualified him from serving as both king and priest for the people of God.

As we look at all of Scripture, then, with Jesus and his work for God's people at the center, we can see how this sinful failure of King Saul points us forward to the saving success of King Jesus. After all, he is the King who is also the perfect high priest for God's people, and his sacrifice is accepted because he is sinless and perfectly worthy! In other words, while the holy God rejects Saul's sacrifice, he accepts the sacrifice for sins offered by our perfect King Jesus. This means that Jesus's death on the cross for our sins—the great sacrifice—really secures our forgiveness and salvation. Saul's failure reveals the need for Jesus and points us ahead to the way he succeeds in every place Saul failed.

1 Kings 10:1–13

We come now to yet another key passage in the Old Testament—one that can be seen as teaching about the high point of the kingdom of Israel. First Kings 10 shows us the splendor of the reign of King Solomon. There is peace in the kingdom, and a glorious palace has been built for this wise king. Many of God's promises to his people are coming true, as the queen of Sheba comes to visit Solomon and goes away blessed by her time with him. But as we will see, even this glorious picture is only a shadow of all that is still to come.

READ!

Read 1 Kings 10:1–13 carefully at least twice. Consider the parts of God's promise to Abraham many years earlier—the promise of a people, of a land, and of blessing to him and to all nations (Gen. 12:1–3). How are these promises coming true in this passage? How does the fulfillment of these promises point ahead to the greater King and kingdom yet to come?

This is a beautiful passage. As Solomon and God's people enjoy the blessings of living in the land God has given to them, the queen of Sheba comes from her far-away nation and is awed by the wisdom and wealth of Solomon. God's promise to Abraham is all coming true.

So if we study and interpret this passage without the cross tool, what will we come up with? Well, we will see the fulfillment of the promise to Abraham—and will probably basically stop there. We will consider the ways that God has brought his people into the land, giving them victory over their enemies. We will see the way that he has made the Israelites into a great people, over whom he has placed this wise king.

Finally, we will focus on the great blessing that God has given to his people—a blessing that is even extending now to the nations around them, as God promised to Abraham. So even without the cross tool, we will still basically get the main point. We will focus on the faithfulness of God to keep his promises and the amazing blessings that he is now raining down on his people in the land of Israel. But what will we have missed?

When we ask ourselves how Jesus would teach this passage to his disciples, we begin to see that we need to consider its relationship to *him*.

How does this passage point us to Jesus and the gospel? It shows us a faint yet glorious picture of the eternal kingdom of Jesus, the true King, which has not yet come to pass. We know from the very next chapters of 1 Kings that just as Solomon's kingdom is at its height, it will begin to crumble quickly under the rule of his foolish son. The glory of this kingdom is short-lived, and it is not the final hope for God's people. Yet it is still a sign that God is keeping his promises to Abraham; there is simply much more to come through Jesus Christ. King Solomon's glory, and the glory of the kingdom under him, is meant to stir hopeful faith in our hearts for the eternal kingdom of the one greater than Solomon: King Jesus, who will rule forever over a people who will never die, but will live in an eternal kingdom that will never crumble.

So the cross tool reminds us that even the glorious reign of Solomon is not God's goal for his people. He has an even greater eternal kingdom for them, and it will be ruled not by Solomon but by his own Son.

Ezra 3

For our final practice text, let's turn to the book of Ezra. This book records events very near the end of the Old Testament period, even though it is not situated at the end of the Old Testament in the Bible. The people have returned to the land of Israel after the exile. In Ezra 3, we learn about the Israelites' efforts to rebuild the temple, which was destroyed during the Babylonian invasion, when many of the people were taken away into captivity. There is something in this passage, as you will see, that drives us ahead toward Jesus Christ—the one who will be the far greater temple for God's people.

READ!

Read the entirety of Ezra 3 carefully and thoughtfully, making observations as you go. Think about the positive picture that is presented as God's people celebrate the rebuilding of their place of worship. Think also about the negative part of the picture, revealed in verse 12. How might that point you to the gospel?

As we approach the end of the Old Testament story in this passage from Ezra, we see God keeping his promises to his people. The exile has ended and they are returning to the land to rebuild all that was destroyed by the Babylonians. This passage tells us of the reconstruction of the temple; it is a great day for God's people.

If we do not put the cross tool to work in our study of Ezra 3, we will probably see this as a good passage for motivating people to work, build, and labor for God's glory. The Israelites, after all, are restoring what has been lost and are rebuilding the place of worship, where they will offer sacrifices and hear God's word taught. This is also a passage about God's faithfulness to his people; he is keeping his promise to bring them back into the land and to restore them after seventy years in exile (Jer. 25:12).

But what happens when we put the cross tool to work in this passage? Is there a path to the gospel that we must take as we study this passage?

The clearest path to the gospel comes in verse 12—a surprising verse that mentions weeping in the midst of the celebration of the temple's completion. Who is weeping? It is the old men—the ones who remember the glory and splendor of the old temple of Solomon. Even as the young people are cheering about the laying of the foundation for the rebuilt temple, the old men weep, because they realize that this new temple will never be as glorious as the old one. They are discovering that the splendors of the age of Solomon will not be restored. Things will never return to the glorious heights of Israel's earthly past.

In the midst of a passage of celebration, we are forced to see that God's people need to set their hopes on something more than a physical temple. This building will not be the answer; they need to start hoping in a far greater meeting place between God and sinful people. Ultimately, Jesus will come and declare that he himself is God's true temple (John 2:18–22). He is the meeting place between God and sinful man; they meet at the cross, through his final sacrifice for sin.

When we put the cross tool to work in Ezra 3, we find that the rebuilt temple only causes us to look for something even better, which is still to come in the Bible story.

REVIEW

Congratulations on coming to the end of yet another chapter and learning to apply this sixth and final tool. During this chapter, you have learned about the cross tool and have put it to work in the study and application of several passages from the Old Testament. You have gained insights into how this tool can remind you to see the gospel as the center of the Bible, and how this perspective makes an impact on your study of every part of it. As you can see from your suggested memory verses in Luke 24, Jesus himself reads the Bible this way. After he rose from the dead, he took time to show his disciples that his life, death, and resurrection fulfill all of the Law, the Prophets, and the Psalms. So when we put the cross tool to work, we are trying to read and study the Bible the way that Jesus did.

Remember that the cross tool can help us avoid moralism and legalism, which are two common ways people apply the Old Testament. It also helps us find grace instead of guilt in our Bible reading and study, helps us keep a proper view of the Bible as Christ-centered, and enables us to see the Bible as one unified story. Finally, keep in mind that some passages point to the gospel through typology, others by the patterns of God's saving work in the world, others by showing the need for the salvation of Jesus, and still others by Old Testament prophecies and promises.

PRAY!

As you close this chapter—and this book—in prayer, spend some time talking to God about a cross-centered and gospel-grounded interpretation of his word. Ask him to help you always remember that the Bible is all about the gospel—the salvation that he has offered freely to sinful human beings through the death and resurrection of his Son. Pray that he would always help you study his word with this central story in mind.

CONCLUSION

We've really only scratched the surface of our training in biblical hermeneutics in this book (the careful work of interpreting and applying God's word). But I hope that you'll emerge from your engagement with this resource equipped with *six distinct tools* that you can and will bring with you to your study of the Bible—whether on your own, in small groups, or as you prepare to teach God's word to others. I want to encourage you to put on your metaphorical hermeneutical tool belt in the days to come as you continue to grow as a student of God's word.

With every passage of Scripture:

1. Use the *context* tool—noting the historical, literary, and canonical context of the biblical passage you are studying.
2. Use the *courtroom* tool—committing to say neither more nor less than what Scripture says.
3. Use the *crux* tool—making sure that you are studying the passage in light of the purpose—and main theme—of the book in which it is contained.

4. Use the *construction* tool—carefully discerning the intentional structure and shape the author has given to the passage.
5. Use the *clarity* tool—seeking to leave behind your personal perspectives and agendas, and allowing the biblical text to speak for itself.
6. Use the *cross* tool—always studying the Bible in light of its central climax: the person and work of Jesus Christ, the Savior and Lord.

May God bless you as you study, discuss, and learn to teach his wonderful inspired word—for his glory and for the good of his people.

GENERAL INDEX

SCRIPTURE INDEX

Available from the Theology Basics Series

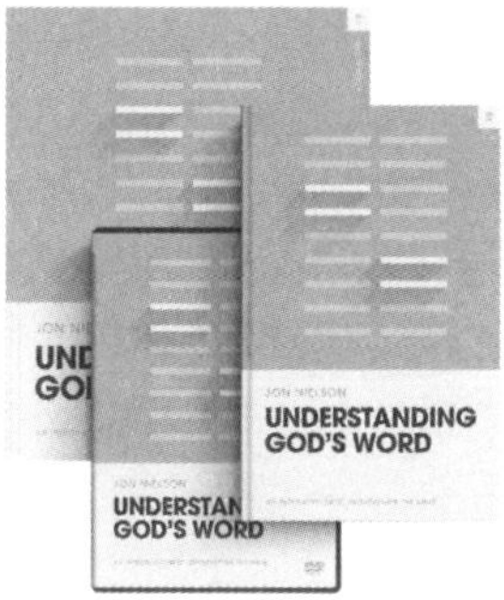

The Theology Basics series is a collection of books, workbooks, and videos designed to provide an accessible introduction to the study of biblical truth—systematic theology, biblical theology, and biblical interpretation.

For more information, visit **crossway.org**.